Echoes of Yorkshire

A Century-Old Diary
Volume 1 (1909-1934)
I, Timmus

R G Thackray

Edited by Stephen G. Liddle

For Grandad Tim,

Thank you for your words which can now echo for generations to come.

Preface

Richard Graham Thackray, or Tim to everyone who knew him, was my Grandad.

Having re-discovered the wonderful musings of my dear departed grandad, I took it upon myself to digitise the memoir of his life. Everyone who has read his private books has said the same thing, "It's great. Someone should publish this!" And I agree; it is a fascinating story.

Within contains the life of a young man growing up almost a century ago. It was a period when The Great War (or World War One, as it would later be known) was still fresh in people's minds. His parents managed to profit from those times and he grew up in fairly affluent surroundings. Though his diaries are long gone, he took the time to type-up and bind several books detailing his life in the first half of the 20th century. This work gives us an accurate and accessible insight into an ordinary middle-class man's life during this part of history.

I have found it amazing how much, even a century later, that we still have the same lives, issues, thoughts, relationships and problems as Grandad faced back then.

Stephen G. Liddle (Grandson)

To help you, dear reader, I have added extra information to inform and educate in this fashion: *[italics]*

Richard Graham Thackray

Looking Backwards

All of us, I suppose, have some common geographical reality - in as much as we are catalogued by Birth Certificates, Passports, and relations, so on and so forth. Earliest recollections, however, are rather more intimate. Mine are just pleasantly vague.

Ah, you will say, Tim has been reading Robert Graves' "Good-bye to all that". Quite correct; I have, and I enjoyed it so much that I think it would be rather fun to see what I can remember.

[The book 'Good-Bye to All That', was written in 1929, with the author aged 34. 'Good-Bye to All That' details Graves's life from his upper-middle-class childhood in England to his service as a military officer in World War I, and on to his first few years as a veteran. This memoir provides a candid account of military service tinged by Graves's poetic sensibilities. Future volumes will see Tim Thackray taking a similar route and this book serves the same template.]

My early infancy is easy to record, because it is a blank. Somehow, I don't think I was altogether a satisfactory child, being the only one, I suffered from the usual complaint:

"Enfant Gate,

Vertu Du Pâtée

Non, ma mere,

Il est trop sale...."

[*Rough French Translation: 'Spoiled child, Virtue Of The Pie, No, my mother, It's too dirty....' Possibly a reference to a spoiled child demanding the food they want and refusing to eat anything else you give to them.*]

I had many governesses, but none of them had either the requisite patience or skill to establish themselves for long at "Four Gables"; so, in desperation, I was packed off to Miss Hoe's Kindergarten, where we learned to count red, yellow, and blue beads, and messed about with crayons and Plasticine; and, I suppose, learned in some measure, the meaning of discipline.

I suppose I was quite a normal child in as much as I climbed trees, threw stones for conkers, played tricks, truant, and loved sweets.

Ever since I have been able to walk I have shown a great inclination for playing with, and making fires everywhere and anywhere. One incident I well remember - that was raking out the nursery fire on to the floor, with disastrous results. Mother can tell you of many similar incidents - making huts in trees; each adorned with a fire-place. Once, when I was about four, when we were staying in Scarborough, I can remember being hauled from my cosy cot; being wrapped in an eiderdown, then taken onto "The Spa" to watch the firework display. I have been an especially "Good Boy" for nearly two whole weeks in order to secure this "Very Big Favour"!

There is an amusing incident that Mother sometimes tells. Once, when she was taking me down to Bournemouth, we had to change at Birmingham. When walking along the platform, Tim was heard to exclaim in a loud childish voice "Oh! Mummie, look, that engine is doing its 'ones' in the station." The engine was, of course, merely running off some surplus water, or condensed steam.

I suffered, in common with most other children, from the usual childish complaints - tonsils, adenoids or both. So, in the spring of 1914, I was yanked off to The Belmont Nursing Home in Leeds, and they were duly removed by Bill Pinder one Sunday morning. Funny how one can remember little incidents, but I remember, as if it were only yesterday, Bill Pinder saying, "Come on, old man", or something like that, just as I was about to "fade out" with the chloroform as the Town Hall clock struck eleven.

Luxury of every conceivable kind, and every possible attention helped to restore the child's health. After about ten days I returned to my little bedroom, with its brightly checked wallpaper at "Four Gables".

After six years these palmy days came to an end, and I was packed off to boarding school - Grosvenor House, Harrogate. My parents doubtless hoping and fervently praying that I should be a better lad. I stayed at Miss Birds until I was eight, and the only outstanding event which happened during those two years was that I tasted the tree of knowledge, and I admit without shame, that its taste was, at the time, sweet; but I suppose that it was only natural, because there's a period in every normal growing up when a boy is quite bi-sexual: If there is a strong pull either one way or another, and if the boy is highly sexed, he is liable to let himself go in what is considered an abnormal way. Though, at the time, it is not abnormal for him. People do create such a fearful howl over it. It is so unnecessary! The thing is a semi-natural phrase, and there's no need to get hysterical about it. Boys have been growing-up ever since the world began, and we have solved the problem, and always will - for ourselves in our own way.

Yes, on the whole I had a remarkably good time when I was in Harrogate. To learn anything never for one moment entered my head. My reports confirmed this. Somehow, I managed to contract Measles, or Chicken-pox nearly every term, and being in the "San", we were allowed much free-time in which to follow our thoughts. I spent most of my time in going for long walks to Birk Cragg. I shall never forget those walks - birds nesting or "tadpolling". I have often meant to go back and have another look at the Craggs, but I know that if I did, those happy memories would only become an illusion. During the War period they were used as an open rifle range. We loved to rummage behind the enormous targets, where we found all sorts of odd things...

Then fishing or catching dragon-flies, with my schoolmates Sam and Jim Bird, and Jim Dryden. Another great attraction was the Tuck Shop, which was at the head of the Craggs; once when Dryden and I paid a visit, we unfortunately lost all count of time, and did not reach school until after dark, when they were about to send search parties out for us. The place was in an uproar, with the result that we both had our first experience of corporal punishment. No further comment is necessary!

In the spring of 1919, I was removed to another "Prep" School - "Southcliffe", Filey. My parents not daring to send me there during hostilities; the civilian population suffered a nasty shock at the bombardment of Scarborough, during the latter part of 1917.

[On September 4th, 1917, a German submarine surfaced in Cayton Bay. It had been a glorious summers day. The sea was flat on Scarborough's South Bay beach and the visitors were enjoying the early evening sun. The German u-boat spotted the British minesweeping fleet in the bay. They took advantage of surprise and opened fire with their guns. The minesweepers were basically armed trawlers crewed almost entirely by fishermen and had become a regular sight in the bay. It took them a few minutes to react to this attack. The submarine bombardment lasted between 10 and 15 minutes. When the minesweepers weighed anchor and started to return fire, the submarine quickly submerged and disappeared. The attack left 3 dead and 6 injured - all civilians].

I was an immediate success at "Southcliffe", and I enjoyed myself tremendously. Many things I shall live over again; Following the Hounds, Wrecks; bowing to His Majesty The Yellow Peril; Stars; and Stripes; and Strawberries; and standing on the form; and Slacks, and swims on hot summers Sunday afternoons. I had a topping lot of pals! Dick Sugden for riding - those memorable rides to Flamborough with old David Burr's horses. Poor fellow, he's dead now. I'm sorry, for David was a sportsman of the old school.

Then, those pre-B.B.C. days, when Ralph used to give us the Sunday afternoon 'Concerts from the Hague' when we congratulated each other on what we had heard, and really all we heard were some atmospherics mingled with a little shipping morse, and much crackling.

Those walks that Miss Palmer took us into the Wilderness, where she used to read amongst others which I can still remember were "The Three Hostages", the "Thirty-nine Steps", and "At the Villa Rose".

['The Three Hostages' is the fourth of five Richard Hannay novels by the Scottish author John Buchan, first published in 1924 by Hodder & Stoughton, London. 'The Thirty-Nine Steps' is a 1915 adventure novel by the Scottish author John Buchan, first published by William Blackwood and Sons, Edinburgh. 'At the Villa Rose' is a 1910 detective novel by the British writer A. E. W. Mason.]

Those hot summer afternoons, when the air was filled with the lazy buzz of bees, the intoxicating smell of

Meadow Sweet, and other wild flowers, together with that of newly mown hay. And far, far away in the distance one hears the rumble of the waves against the rocks of the Brigg. We used to lie in bathing costumes on top of the cliffs by the Aeroplane slope. Gad, what a sight; miles of golden sands, stretching away to the cliffs of Speighton, Bempton, and Flamborough, the latter being hardly visible in the haze. Then there were those School picnics at Hunmanby Gap. Hockey on the sands. Walks to Filey Church, over the Golf Links, complete in 'Bum Freezers' *[a short jacket worn by men]*, Bengies *[a balm for aches and pain]*, and those dreaded Eton Collars *[a large stiff formal collar worn over a normal collar]* when, like good little well-behaved boys we used to sit and listen to The Reverend Canon Cooper, who is perhaps, better known to the world as 'The Walking Parson' preach his famous sermon about the golden salmon on the Church Tower. I enjoyed those sermons. About this time, I had an attack of great religious fervour. I went crazy on candles, candlesticks, and crucifixes. This, however, soon passed.

[Quite a famous character during this period, Arthur Neville Cooper AKA 'The Walking Parson' travelled every European country (excluding Russian territories) with only a small knapsack and a Bible. Filey church has a good history on this chap. He served at Filey's St. Oswald's Church from 1880 until 1935. He decided reluctantly to retire due to failing eyesight and saddened by the fact he could no longer read the Bible. On his retirement he decided to move from Filey to Scarborough "as it wouldn't be fair to the next man. I want to give him a clear field". This

demonstrates what a thoughtful and caring man he seemed to have been. He put down his great health to "taking a cold bath every morning" and all his walking – "the man who walks is the man who is well". His sage advice on walking is "I have learnt that there is one way to walk without trouble: that is to pour whisky in your boots"! "The Walking Parson" died in 1943 and there is a memorial plaque to this remarkable man by the altar of St Oswald's Church, Filey to commemorate this special incumbent who served them for over 55 years.]

In common with other children who have the misfortune to be an only child, I was very spoilt during the holidays, I was more or less allowed to run wild. This was rather foolish, as I was to realise some years later.

However, for the most part, Dad used to be a good pal to me. I cannot really imagine myself at the age of 40, with a wayward and irresponsible young son of my own doing the things we did together. Going up the village, for instance, visiting the houses of absolute strangers, and paying typical school-boyish pranks on them; such as knocking on their doors, and running away as fast as our legs would carry us. Another of our torments would be to tie a button to some black cotton, which was fixed to the wooden crossbar of a window with a drawing pin, the button hanging downwards about afoot. Then by tying some more cotton to the button and leading it to some well concealed place; just out of reach of the irate householder. The fun would begin by letting the button fall repeatedly against the glass. The poor distracted victim would come to the window many times to complete our merriment.

Perhaps the best of the lot was to fasten, very securely, both the door-handles and knockers on a semi-detached house, then knock on both the doors simultaneously. Oh, what fun... I could ramble on for hours.

I shall always remember what the "old Man" said a little later on when I went to Wrekin - with regard to smoking, drinking, and swearing. He said: "....If I forbid you to smoke, I know you'll only disobey me. You would go to the bottom of the garden and have a cigarette just for the sake of being mischievous; so I'm only going to ask you as man-to-man to smoke as little as you can, because it isn't really being clever or manly". Unfortunately, he never mentioned those things that every boy comes up against sooner or later, and it's generally sooner. Had he done so; it would, in all probability have saved me some embarrassing moments later on. When I was thirteen, and Barbara *[his sister]* came so unexpectedly into the world, I was the least curious, I sort of took it all for granted. I was so surprised in fact, that I cannot recall or analyse my feelings, and thought (if any).

I would like to mention that old Gowe (The Rev.A.H. Gowe M.A., the headmaster of "Southcliffe"), managed to succeed in teaching me many things; when to write O and Oh, also the Latin Syntax, and the Irregular and Anomalous Verbs inside out, and partially succeeded with his pet motto... "Manners maketh man". Now that I have said goodbye to school (it seems years ago now), it has struck me how delightful it is about our Prep Schools, we used to call each other by our Christian names - a thing which, if we attempted to do at our public schools, would have been very "taboo", and laid ourselves open to an unmerciful ragging *[To tease, annoy or torment]*.

Anyway when the time came to say "Goodbye" to dear old Southcliffe, I believe I cried.

The First Corner

The remaining years of my school-life were spent at Wrekin College, Wellington, Shropshire, [*Described at the time as: one of the most widely known and popular educational establishments for gentlemen's sons in the Midlands*] and I have a vague feeling that I was rather a failure. I was certainly unpopular, and some of my friends were of the wrong type. I don't say all by a long way. From the moment I arrived at Wellington, I suffered an oppression of spirit, that even now I hesitate to recall in its full intensity. The trouble did not begin my first-term, as I was left very much to my own devices, as most new kids are. It was in my second term that the trouble started. Wrekin's chief interests, in common I suppose with other public schools, apparently "were" games and romantic friendships, and, unfortunately I was bored with athletics, and my eyes were not blue enough for me to be a success in the other direction. So I was generally looked upon as a 'wet-bob'. Schoolwork was generally despised by everyone, and I joined forces in the common effort against the majority of the masters - so consequently I was disliked by them also. I believe, the new head Mr. W. M. Gordon ("Maxie"), has done a great deal to change this state of affairs. Mr. Gordon went to Wrekin the same term as myself.

During the summer I took up swimming, perhaps, more seriously than I had attempted previously. The net result was that I got some of the Life Saving certificates and the Copper medal - all duly presented by the Head. The result of this enthusiasm, was that I was often excused those dreaded 'nets'. I think I'm right in saying that during the whole of my career at Wrekin I did not play more than a dozen games of cricket. And it is one of the things I have lived to regret. I also made a pretty feeble effort at carpentry in order to avoid house games. When this ruse was discovered, life in the House Room became rather too warm to be pleasant. Then as a final coup I took up marksmanship on the open range on The Wrekin - with considerable success. The beauty of this move lay in being allowed a bicycle, and a free permit through the town, which was normally out of bounds, up to Forest Glen for Cigarettes and ham and egg teas(!). Another feature, was that one could roam to one's heart's content over The Ercall [Pronounced Arc-al, it is a small hill near Wellington] and Wrekin, and enjoy a peaceful smoke, without the remotest chance of being caught... and so forget some drudgery of school. The most remarkable blackberries grow on the Wrekin.

In the eyes of the House and School press, I was a tick, in fact a bloody little tick, and in consequence I was generally to be found working overtime - either fagging or completing imports, or putting things straight after a ragging. One of the favourite forms of imposition in vogue was to make us learn by heart something out of Palgreave's immortal "Golden Treasury" - a mere sixty lines or so. Whilst the master used to take particular delight in handing out 'punishment drill' ad lib. Punishment Drill consisted of half or an hours absolute hell, under the skilful direction of Sgt. Maj. Robinson. This form of punishment, which took place on Wednesday afternoons, was reserved for the sole use of Masters, who were never known to fail in making full use of their advantage. Perhaps it was a good thing.

I have always been stubborn when roused. On one occasion, either I wouldn't or couldn't do an imposition. I may have even refused to do it point blank, I forget which now. But the result was that I was referred to the Head; the bubble burst, and I was soundly beaten by the Head himself, so in a way I was quite unique for not many of my fellows, received that treatment. It was, however, of no avail. I was just the same afterwards. The Head did do one thing for me and for which I shall be everlastingly grateful, and that is that he taught me to write a reasonably legible hand. Wrekin, however, failed utterly and completely in its efforts to teach me the finer points of spelling.

I was notoriously slack in The O.T.C. *[Officer Training Corp, established in 1908 and designed to attract young men into the army]*. And like many other things, it was one which I was to regret in later years. Three scenes in particular stand out very vividly. The first was the Commanding Officer 'Old Split' (B. C. W. Johnson, now O.B.E.), when criticising the parade suddenly came out with ".....had it not been for the left marker in No 2 Platoon of "A" Company continually fidgeting with his equipment it would have been an excellent parade...." And with the recollection of the incident I can almost feel the gaze of some two hundred pairs of eyes then fixed on me. The second still hurts. The Old Man (at my request) had written to Mr. Johnson, asking if I might be excused Camp at Strensall on the grounds that I was not strong enough. He replied to me personally in front of the whole class; by saying that he was only too pleased to be able to do this, as he had intended in getting me excused in my case, as my presence would have let down the whole company. Titters round the class.

The third sad moment was when the Cert "A" results were posted, There were only two failures, and I was the first with 29%, instead of the requisite 33%.

I must be fair to myself. There are two sides to every picture. The contrasting scene was my being cheered by the whole school, when I managed to pull off one of the Inter-House Boxing competitions, and which gave me a place in the School Boxing Team. It was quite the jolliest day I'd spent at Wrekin, but, unfortunately this service was soon forgotten by the House. It was not even mentioned in the "Valete" notices in The Wrekinian. I have just unearthed an old autograph book - even Wrekin had its sense of humour. On one page, Herbert Bowman had written an original epigram... "You can never tell a sausage by its skin", and which after all is quite true.

[The School used to publish a magazine each term called "The Wrekinian" which contained a record of School activity each term.

In the Wrekinian No 12, (Christmas 1924) he is recorded as playing in the Under 15 rugby for his House against Norman House - Hanover lost.

Tim also appears in No. 16, page 21 (Easter 1926):

"THE ATHENAEUM.

This term has seen the passing of the Junior Archaeological Society, and the formation in its place of the Athenaeum, which has taken over its membership and its traditions. Four papers were given during the term. R. G. Thackray gave an interesting account of the Pharos of Alexandria ; R. A. R. Howatt treated well, and from a new angle, of the Tomb of Tutankhamen ; Mr. W. F. Higgs-Walker illustrated his paper on Thebes with many photos taken during a tour in Egypt. For the last paper, " A Defence of Mediaeval Builders'. We were able to welcome Mr. R. G. Gibbon's return to us."

He again appears in No 58 (1940) as an Old Wrekinian on active service as a Lance Corporal in the Yorkshire Regiment.

Finally he appears in the Old Wrekinian magazine in 1988: Richard Graham Thackray (Hanover 1922-26) records 'I have lived a full and happy life, now being 78. I must always thank W.M.G. (Walter Maxwell Gordon - former Headmaster) for teaching me to write'. (His writing is STILL immaculate! Ed.)

Thanks to Peter K Brown, Archivist, Wrekin College for this information.]

Doubtless I was unappreciative of the hard knocks, and character training that public schools are supposed to provide. With regard to exams, I was always a failure; and only passed one (and that by the skin of my teeth) in my life. I have not even the School Cert. or Matric *[a former school examination, which was replaced by the General Certificate of Education (Ordinary Level), now superseded by the General Certificate of Secondary Education.]* to my credit. In fact I hardly earned a thing at Wrekin. Father was generally too busy absorbed with himself, or having a good time to worry about that side of my education. As a matter of fact the family were just coming to the end of their hey-day. In common with all other capitalists, they made so much blasted money during the War they did not know which way to spend it fast enough. *[The family made their fortune in the leather trade. In World War 1 - known then, as The Great War - leather was used in military footwear and for horses saddles and bridles, amongst other things.]* The first thing they did was to fill the house with a rowdy crowd of officers - of the eat-drink-and-be-merry-for-tomorrow-we-die brigade, they drank the old man's whiskey as though it had been water.

The next thing they did was to take the old Hall at Newlaithes - God! What a wonderful old place. Its ballroom was the scone of many gay parties *[when 'gay' meant 'cheerful' or 'carefree']*. Its magnificent old gardens were mellowed with age. It was certainly a show place. Without exaggeration my parents must have spent thousands in getting the place to the perfection it finally became. It was very dilapidated when they took it over. As you would expect when a man is foolish enough to be so lavish with his hospitality as he was, he attracted a very large circle of friends, who knew what they wanted and saw that they got it.

However, the screw had begun to tighten, that is why I left Wrekin when I was an immature seventeen. The Bank had had to step in at Newlay by taking a big debenture, covering an indiscretion of Uncle Richard Thackray. A few months after I had left Wrekin, the family were forced to say 'au revoir' to Newlaithes. They moved their worldly possessions to a very much smaller house, "Hill Rise", not very far away, and with practically no garden. To me it was a very sad moment, having to say good-bye to Newlaithes, for I'd had some wonderful times there.

In England, parents of the governing classes virtually finish all intimate life with their children at the age of about seven or eight, and any attempt on their part to institute home life into school life is resented by the child.

Generally speaking, school life becomes the reality, and the home life the illusion. For instance a school boy when at home on holiday will often, quite unconsciously address his Mother "Oh, I say Matron...", or to his Father "Yes, Sir...", as though he were a master. I've done it often myself.

For a period I tried to get some relief in Chapel, but only found more drudgery - chiefly in the form of Choir practices, which became very boring. In the end I went so far as to get excused Chapel every other week. The excuse being - organ pumping. Thus during the sermon on Sundays, one could stroll unmolested, and hands in pockets (what rare luxury) peacefully over the school lawns, which were normally out of bounds; and if wet; read a book in one of the comfy chairs in the Vestry. For a whole term I concentrated all my thoughts on religion, and eagerly looked forward to the ceremony of Confirmation as a spiritual climax. So when the time came, and The Lord Bishop of Lichfield completed the laying on of hands, I found the Holy Ghost did not descend upon me, nor was I filled with the learning and many tongues. In fact nothing spectacular happened. I was bound to, and did, feel a reaction.

Until recently, I had still kept a few letters from my parents, which I received when at Wrekin; but I have destroyed most of them, because every time I looked at them it made me feel guilty of unworthiness. You can tell what the old man thought about me when he went so far as to borrow money from Uncle Tom Wright (probably knowing at the time that he would never be required to pay it back), in order that he might keep his son at a public school, costing some £200 a year in fees alone *[That would be the equivalent of about £15,000 today]*. His son, I'm sorry to say never adequately thanked him. At the end of the last term when 'the parents' came down to the Sports and to take their prodigal home - all he said was "...Well! Thank God that's over with". And that was all they got for their trouble.

There are just two more memories of Wrekin. One was the Head's "goodbye" in my last Report. It was this: "...A good lad, but apparently silly. He must grow up. In all his dealings with me, I find him pleasant. Has something in him, and should do well. I am more than sorry to say "Good-bye"... and I wish him all success".

The other - the immortal 'Heads Hour'. I can see now, the grey-haired Maxie, pacing the classroom, those fine strong lines about his face denoting such strength of character that unable him to impart that determination to a young man, that would make him say, "I'll fight for success - for all that is beautiful; and to that end I'll never stop."

I have just unearthed an old exercise book, which contained notes that were taken during the 'Head's Hour'. I have set them down here in the same order that presumably Maxie gave them to us. I am taking all his statements as correct. I have never bothered to authenticate them - sheer blinking laziness, I know:

Important dates in English History.

1500.
The Revival of Learning,
Invention of Printing,
Discovery of America,
The Reformation.

1850.
The Discovery of Steam.

Relevant = on the subject
Naive = Childish, and simple,
Solecism = a foolish mistake in manners or speech.

1757 = The Battle of Plassey,
1857= The Indian Mutiny.

Read 'The Life of Warren Hastings'. *[Warren Hastings (1732-1818) was one of the key figures in establishing the East India Company's empire in Asia. As the first Governor-General of Bengal, he played a crucial role in consolidating the territories won by Robert Clive at the Battle of Plassey in 1757.]*

Don't talk people down.
Don't use blotting paper,

Must look up:-
(1) What St. James said about the tongue, *[The tongue is like a tiny flame from hell. Uncontrolled speech can set aflame an entire forest worth of sin, and sets our own bodies on fire as well (verses 5-6). The tongue is like a wild animal that is nearly impossible to tame (verse 7). The tongue is like poison (verse 8)]*
(2) Why are the following known in Ireland. Cromwell, James 2, and William. *[James II, the Catholic King, restored hope in Ireland by appointing Catholics to governmental positions. He hoped to scrap Cromwellian Land Law, but unfortunately for Ireland, he became embroiled in a battle for the throne with William of Orange (William III). In 1690, 'King Billy' defeated James II in the Battle of the Boyne, near Drogheda, and took control of Ireland. The battle is still celebrated annually by Orangemen on July 12, during the 'marching season', and many murals depict him sitting astride his white charger, on the walls of 'Loyalist' housing estates.]*

(3) Shakespeare: Romances = "As you like it", and "The Tempest". Both these end in reunion.

Polonius said…"I have a daughter".

The most progressive state in S. America is The Argentine.

Corfu is the most important Ionian Island.

The Channel Islands are:-
Jersey,
Alderney,
Sark,
Guernsey,
Herm, and
Jethou.

To be discussed :- Great Railway Disasters.

Mr. Brearley = the greatest bowler in the world.
[Walter Brearley was a businessman in the cotton trade who gained fame as the last amateur fast bowler in England in the decade before the First World War.]

Wisden = Cricket Record.
[Wisden Cricketers' Almanack, or simply Wisden, colloquially the Bible of Cricket, is a cricket reference book published annually in the United Kingdom.]

Lucretious = Latin Poet.

The Magnesium Stone = the first magnet

.....Port always from left to right.

The most excitable hunting is to be found in Ireland.

We are the greatest people on earth.

To forgo, is to go without,
and to forego, is to go before.

Look through Hymn 339.
[My Country, 'Tis of Thee
*   •   1. My country, 'tis of thee,*
*   Sweet land of liberty,*
*   Of thee I sing;*
*   Land where my fathers died,*
*   Land of the pilgrims' pride,*
*   From ev'ry mountainside*
*   Let freedom ring!*
*   •   2. My native country, thee,*
*   Land of the noble free,*
*   Thy name I love;*
*   I love thy rocks and rills,*
*   Thy woods and templed hills.*
*   My heart with rapture thrills*
*   Like that above.*
*   •   3. Let music swell the breeze*
*   And ring from all the trees*
*   Sweet freedom's song;*
*   Let mortal tongues awake;*
*   Let all that breathe partake;*
*   Let rocks their silence break,*
*   The sound prolong.*
*   •   4. Our fathers' God, to thee,*
*   Author of liberty,*
*   To thee we sing;*

30

Long may our land be bright
With freedom's holy light.
Protect us by thy might,
Great God, our King!]

There are 5 periods in English Literature:-

1552-1599 Spencer
1564-1593 Marlowe
1564-1610 Shakespeare.
1608-1674 Milton
1770-1850 Wordsworth

Try to cultivate a mind that does <u>NOT</u> give way when life is steep. <u>AND</u> when life goes well <u>NOT</u> lose your head.

I shall be a DUD if I don't make an effort.

Force and determination must also be developed.

I must learn to say "No", and mean it, and I must choose decent society.

Reading and punctuality are essential... and they are not natural habits.

<u>DON'T WASTE TIME</u>.

I must learn to look after my body, Washing, and Physical Training.

I <u>must</u> develop Sharpness

Be as decent a chap as you can

Try to learn as much as you can

Don't <u>think</u> every-body are rotters,

George IV was mad.

British workmen are the finest in the world.

Don't talk about others behind their backs.

THINK OF MY OUTPUT.

Don't let your mind wander.

To give some idea of my mentality at the age of 16, here are a few typical entries out of my Diary, which I kept religiously, until I left school. The Diaries have since been destroyed:

<u>SUNDAY, JANUARY 25th, 1925 (School)</u>.

Felt a bit homesick.
Sold clock to Dudley Ship for 2/-.
The Cross-word craze is intense.
Charlie Offer preached a rotten sermon.
After Chapel went to a Junior Literary Society meeting, was elected Hon. Sec.

MONDAY, JANUARY 26th 1925. (School).

Nearly late for breakfast. Finished dressing while sprinting up from Newlands after first bell. Went to the Head for writing class after lunch, and asked him if I could take extra Maths. In consequence I was ticked off; and told that I had to do it in my spare time. Terrific wind, and it rained all afternoon. Did not play rugger. Had a decent letter from home. I hate Cleland and Whitehouse.

TUESDAY, JANUARY 27th 1925 (School).

Damn Karki and puttees.
Damn all O.T.C. *[Officer Training Corp]* Parades.
And Damn The War Office.
Got ragged by Marfell, & Jones F. B. Fight ensued. Got very much worsted.
Hellish Cold.
Had rabbit for lunch.

WEDNESDAY, JANUARY 28th, 1925. (School).

No letters. Drew 10/- pocket money.
Shaw the hellish pre, gave me a terrific impot.
Played rugger for the House Colts. Scored scored a try, Bobbie Byass came up at half-time and said "Well done", Felt bucked.
Had tea with the Junior Field Club, with Jones H.A.O. Then had another tea at the Tuck Shop.

Moved places in Chapel, so that I could sit next to Jim Harrison in the gallery.

THURSDAY, MARCH 19th, (School),1925.

Ripping letter from Mother, Barbara has had her hair bobbed. Madame Tussauds is burnt down in London.
Had a bath, went to the bogs 13 times.
Only 20 more days then home! Cheers.

MONDAY APRIL 27th, 1925. (Holidays)

Got up late. Went to the Dentist. Old Marston tried to take out a tooth with gas, but unfortunately failed. Hurt like hell.
Mr Hindenburg is to be Germany's first President.

TUESDAY, MAY 12th, 1925 (School).

Parade again. I got up early to clean my buttons and equipment. Was put down to play cricket, but as usual managed to get off.
The Swimming baths are being filled.

WEDNESDAY, JUNE 3rd, 1925. (School).

King George V Birthday.
Usual 1/2 holiday.
Glorious Weather.
John T.G.V. and Evans A.Y. are simply great fellows.

Saucy Sue has had another win, *[Saucy Sue (1922 – July 1937) was a British Thoroughbred racehorse and brood-mare, best known for winning two Classics in 1925. At Royal Ascot in June, Saucy Sue was in the Coronation Stakes and started at odds of 1/10.]* and I won 2/6 from Thorpe L.A.

Had a gut of Sardines, and Chocolate Biscuits in the Junior Cloak Room.

SATURDAY, JUNE 27th, 1925 (School)

The most marvellous weather possible.

Went up to the Range *[shooting range on the Ercall]*, and on my way I got a packet of fags. The shooting match is between the School and 'C' Coy of the K.S.L.I. *[King's Shropshire Light Infantry. Throughout its time, the KSLI was involved in many battles and campaigns, and it was arguably during the Great War that the regiment saw the most action.]* I forget who won.

Had a fine tea at Forest Glen *[at the foot of the Wrekin]* afterwards. The Territorials *[Territorial Army - a part-time volunteer part of the British Army]* are great chaps.

Went for a ripping swim in the evening.

Have only played two games of Cricket so far this term. Aren't I lucky? The House Matches have started today. Tudor v Hano, we lost the first innings by 10 runs.

Had a rotten Latin Translation Exam in the morning, but soon forgot this when I got a letter from Dad containing a 10/- note.

[Time for a quick lesson on English currency pre-1971:

35

*A pound (£) was expressed in shillings and pennies.
"Bob" is slang for a shilling (5p in todays money)
1 shilling equalled twelve pence (12d). The Pence
was written as d - from the Roman 'dinarius'.
£1 (one pound) equalled 20 shillings (20s or 20/-)
240 pennies (240d) = £1
Fact: There were 240 pennies to a £ because
originally 240 silver penny coins weighed 1 pound
(1lb).
A sum of £3 12s 6d would be written as £3-12-6, but
a sum of 12s 6d was normally recorded as 12/6.
Amounts less than a pound were also written as:
12/6 meaning 12s-6d
So, Tim's 10/- note meant he got 10s or ten shillings
or the equivalent of over £40 in modern money.]*

THURSDAY, JUNE 23rd, 1926 (School)

The Head tells me I am a bad speller. Spelt 'business' -'buisness', and got badly ticked off.

...and so it goes on.

In the back of my Diary for 1925, there is a list of the books that I managed to struggle through, I say struggle, because I have never been a natural reader - unfortunately, perhaps an inheritance, who knows?

Livingstone: The Master Missionary, *[by Hubert F. Livingstone Wilson]*

The Good Ship "Golden Effort" by Percy F. Westerman. *[Author of, now-dated, 'ripping good yarns']*

The White Feather by P. G. Wodehouse *[Author writes about boxing!]*

Seconds out of the Ring, *[?]*

The Power of the Borgias *[by William Le Queux, 1920]*

Goal *[?]*

Two thousand leagues under the Sea *[by Jules Verne]*

Captain Cain *[by Percy F. Westerman]*

Les Miserables *[by Victor Hugo, 1862]*

The Green Eyes of Bast *[by Sax Rohmer, an early and largely forgotten SF and fantasy author who created Dr. Fu Manchu]*

The Blue Lagoon *[a coming-of-age romance novel written by Henry De Vere Stacpoole, made into a famous movie]*

The Doctor of Pimlico, W. Le Q. *[aka 'The Doctor of Pimlico: Being the Disclosure of a Great Crime' by William Le Queux (pronounced "Q")]*

The Quest of the Black Opals. (Macdonald) *[aka 'The Quest Of The Black Opals A Story Of Adventure In The Heart Of Australia' by Alexander MacDonald, 1908]*

A Study in Scarlet, (Doyle) *[A Study in Scarlet is an 1887 detective novel by British writer Arthur Conan Doyle. The story marks the first appearance of Sherlock Holmes and Dr. Watson, who would become the most famous detective duo in literature.]*

Hushed up! W. Le Q. *[Hushed Up!: A Mystery of London by William Le Queux (1911)]*

Famous Explorers, *[The Kingsway Book of Famous Explorers by Robert James Finch (1923)]*

The Gods of Mars (E.B-R), *[The Gods of Mars by Edgar Rice Burroughs (1913). The second book in the John Carter series]*

The Man about Town, *[by O. Henry (1906)]*

The Red Widow by W. Le Q *[The Red Widow, Or The Death-Dealers of London by William Le Queux (1920)]*

Tales of Long Ago. (Doyle), *[Tales of Long Ago - a volume collecting 13 short stories - by Arthur Conan Doyle (1922)]*

The House of a hundred Horrors! *[?]*

Dreadnoughts of the Air by Percy F. Westerman. *[1914]*

The Phantom Airman. *[by Rowland Walker (1920)]*

The Sub and a Submarine by Percy F. Westerman, *[(1919)]*

The Loom of Youth by Alec Waugh. *[(1917)]*

The Secret Island by Jules Verne, *[The Secret Of The Island is the third book in the 'Mysterious Island' trilogy (The Mysterious Island and Abandoned are the first two), and is related to 20,000 Leagues Under The Sea (1876)]*

The Honourable Jim *[by Baroness Orczy (1924)]*

Hell and High Water, *[?]*

East in the Golden Gain, P.F. Westerman. *[East in the "Golden Gain" by Percy F. Westerman (1925)]*

The Gauntlet of Alceste, *[The Addison Kent Mysteries: The Gauntlet of Alceste by Herbert J. (Hopkins) Moorhouse (1921)]*

Revelations of The Secret Service, W. Le Q., *[by William Le Queux (1911)]*

The 39 Steps, (J.B.), *[The 39 Steps by John Buchan (1915) was also a hit movie and the inspiration for Ian Fleming's James Bond]*

What an assortment. To look through this list only five years later, makes me positively shudder.

"Sixteen to Twenty-one."

...And now I have come to the end of my actual School career. What can I say of Life now that I have finished the instructional part of my Education and just entering the wider field? - Is there nothing more to learn? I have said "Good-bye" to School discipline. How shall I use this new freedom?

Those were my thoughts towards the end of 1926, when I left Wrekin, and whilst on the subject of thoughts and thinking; I wonder in a mild sort of way if my thoughts will continue to be so erratic, and if my powers of concentration will continue to be so spasmodic.

I think there can be no doubt that my instinct for doing things erratically, and my habit of untidy thought is either hereditary, or the result of early environment. I have always been inconsistent, and often mentally weak, in giving way to odd fancies, and little whims, without necessary reasoning.

Sometimes I can get up with the lark as early as 6 a.m. and sometimes it will be a struggle to roll out of bed at 8 a.m. Sometimes if the mood takes me, I will plunge into a cold bath. Ah! But only sometimes. I have a very dogged determination for seeing things to the bitter end, and yet another is that of complete disregard for the value of money, and the inability to save anything.

My parents, for some inexplicable reason, do the most odd things at the most odd moments in life. But not for one moment do I belittle them, far from it, they both have sterling qualities together with one invaluable asset - the ability to be cheerful in the most exasperating circumstances. But they have yet to learn the meaning of the word 'tact'.

I wonder if my train of thought is normal or abnormal? The warming-up period generally requires about half an hour's concentrated effort, then they seem to come in quite a steady flow, and I will go on jogging on the jolly old "typer" at quite a decent speed. But I have yet to devise a satisfactory method of timing my actual output in words per hour.

Shelly tells us that he used to do his best thinking when walking in the woods surrounded by an absolute peace and quietness. At such times, he goes on: "...my thoughts come quite naturally, and without effort".

Graham Wallas, who wrote "The Art of thought", tells us that his best thoughts come when he is in a bath. But I bet that he has never had the moral courage to go into a shop and ask for a waterproofed writing pad.

I have noticed that I can often think with extreme clarity when I am about to start with a feverish cold or chill, and sometimes too, when I have just had a drink or two. However, I bar such luxuries. I should, in all probability, pass out long before I had time to reach out and tabulate my thoughts.

To return to the subject on hand, or as the French could say 'Revenons vos muttons', *[He means 'Revenons à nos moutons' - To return to the subject - Tim's French wasn't perfect]* never, that I can remember, was I asked what I wanted to be. It being always understood that I should carry on the family tradition, and into the Tannery. And so, after a very ordinary holiday, I went, in the Autumn of 1926.

I cannot recall my first impressions of work. On the whole, I think I liked it, though I felt very embarrassed in doing anything in the presence of workmen. My job consisted chiefly of manual labour. The old man insisting on putting me through it from the bottom - somehow it made me feel quite manly. One of the first lessons I was to learn, and learn with considerable bitterness, was the futility of relations in business - constant bickering between brother and brother, and in my case between cousin and cousin, and on more than one occasion, Father and son did not see eye-to-eye about the management of the business - had I just stopped to think. Whilst I was thus employed; my financial balance became very sound, so sound, in fact that I started gambling on "ossess", beginning in the usual way: tanners *[sixpence]*, at first, then bobs *[a shilling]*, then dollars *[5 shillings]*, and so on until it reached sovereigns *[£'s]*. The bubble finally burst when I had lost my last £3 on a horse - which came in second. What if Father got to know that I had run through something like £30 or £40.....? *[Over £3,000 in today's money]* Ye Gods! Anyway rejoice, that I had the good sense to stop and reflect over my rashness. From that day, I can honestly say that I have never been so bold as to even risk an odd bob on a "hoss".

Early in 1926, I experienced rather a novel adventure. The jolly old Trades Union Council decided to have a General Strike - sympathising with the miners. The Country went to the Country for volunteers to carry on the essential services such as transport, et cetera: Immediately I wanted to satisfy an hidden ambition of early childhood... that of being an engine driver! The authorities turned me down on account of my youth. However, after a bit of string pulling, I was accepted by The London Midland and Scottish Railway *[L.M.S.]* as a signalman at Newlay Station, which of course was eminently suitable. I had to present myself for work at the early hour of six, and finishing at two in the afternoon. The work was both pleasant and interesting, probably because it was novel, and the work was not without excitement, and suitable remuneration. My employment with the railway lasted for a couple of weeks. About a month later I received my second medal, this from the Chairman of the L.M.S., Sir Josiah Stamp, together with a very flowery letter - recognising 'my valuable services' in the 'great emergency' . In another bit of the letter it says "...and once again the British race showed that they will not surrender their dearly bought freedom at the dictation of any section of the Community..."

Within a month or two, a very serious blow came upon the family, affecting my whole existence. On Friday evening, July 27th 1927, Father casually announced at tea - when we were on our holiday at Scarborough - that the works at Newlay were going into Voluntary Liquidation, and that shortly we were to be left high and dry. The total deficiency was a trifle over £18,000 *[in todays money, over £1.5 million]*, half of which were unsecured creditors, and the other half as regards debenture holders (i.e. the Bank). The plant, land and machinery stood us to £17,500, but at the subsequent sale realised only £4,500.

I can remember, quite clearly, that the absolute calmness Dad displayed amazed me. Mother and I thought it was not the end of the world, and, indeed, it was not so very far away, because within a few months we were on our beam ends. At one time it looked as though our very home was in danger. Our wealthier relations rallied to our aid splendidly - though not to Dad's thinking.

After two weeks actual unemployment, I was given a position with Messrs, Charles F. Stead & Co. Ltd., of Sheepscar Tannery (formally Messrs. Wilson and Walker). I was still to be a workman, but with a big difference... I was not to be my own master. At Newlay I could have caught the 11.15 to town for a swim at the baths or wander round the tannery to the fields or the river for a peaceful smoke - to forget the whirr of the machinery. Nevertheless, it was a great tonic to be amongst men and machines again. But to work alongside girls was a new and strange experience. Their outlook, and their mentality is truly strange. Girls, like cattle, have some very queer habits.

I worked under a bigger strain during the twelve months I was at Stead's than in any previous period of my life. My daily routine was as follows: I had to get up about 6.15am in order to be there at 8. I was late only three times during the whole twelve months - a pretty fair record! Circumstances forced me to have lunch, which consisted of sandwiches, reclining or sitting on bales of kips *[Kip is the untanned hide of a young or small animal, such as a calf, lamb, or young goat. The leather made from such hide is called kip leather and is softer than cowhide]* in the rough leather warehouse; overlooking some of the filthiest slums ever made. God! how those people smoke, and refuse was everywhere! I only ate my food because I was hungry, the kind of hunger that comes as the result of hard work. It used to grow very monotonous. When I had nothing to do, I used to write poetry. No specimens survive, which is, perhaps, a good thing. The peculiar rhythm of the glazing machines *[for polishing leather]* provided many ideas for metre.

I had not much of a job. My weekly efforts, brought me the meagre sum of 25/- (gross). Out of this, I paid Mother 3/- a week, paid my tram fares (about 5/-), my fees for the Evening Classes, provide myself with a tea for three nights a week; clothe myself, and pay my compulsory State Insurance. Of course it was impossible, because I had to live as well. And so it came to pass that my last £40 went to the place where all good men go.

Work finished at, five, so I made my way towards an old attic in Vicar Lane - which was the den of a local boxer, and put in an hours useful training. I enjoyed myself there. It kept me fit, and was a bit of experience, besides it relieved the monotony.

To me there is an indescribable fascination about boxing - the dual play, the reciprocity, the pain, not felt as pain - calling to mind those grand lines from Masefield's "Everlasting Mercy":-

"Whose never felt the Boxers trim
of brain divinely knit to limb,
Nor felt the whole live body go
One tingling health from top to toe;
Nor taken a punch, nor given a swing,
But just soaked deady round the ring."

I think they're topping. After a hasty rub down, I had to dash off to the Leeds Technical School or to The University for my evening classes. Eventually I arrived home again,

47

invariably dog tired, about ten o'clock. Anyway, the result of going to these classes was that I actually succeeded in getting my Intermediate, City and Guilds for the Manufacture of Leather, which was something.

My keenness for collecting patterns of the fancy leathers made by Steads got the better of me, because for my own amusement I made a collection of these cuttings, and neatly pasted them in a book. I also did a bit of buying and selling - in the vain hope of restoring my forlorn bank balance. To me, I can always get an aesthetic thrill when I look through that book of small leather cuttings that I actually made with my own hands! Not the book, but the Cuttings of Leather, of course. However, to cut the story short; one day Mr. Stead sent for me, and we had a real old row. He was evidently under the impression that these patterns were being sent to Father, who had been appointed works manager of a rival firm - Messrs. T. N. and F. H. Briggs of Leicester - only a few months ago. When I came out of that office I knew that I had turned the corner of my career. For those of us who like to believe in coincidences Mr. Stead was killed a few months later in a motoring accident. I have the last laugh. That night I went home and blubbed. I was numbed. I was frightened, too, for the first time in my life... of Mrs. Grundy. Having kept my job for only twelve months then to "an out-of-work" again. For a few days I just went for long walks to try and forget. Then Mr. Tom Gate told me that I could start for him selling his Chamois Leathers and Sole Bends. I set myself to work with a new or rather renewed vigour. I was to be a salesman, and I kew nothing of the art. Still on looking back, those two years with Mr. Gate were wonderfully pleasant. It is said that experience is the best way to learn. I stuck to it.... and did well. Nothing was too much trouble, be it early or late, work came first. I was allowed to let my imagination take me where it would and though I say it myself, my imagination is rather more fertile than most. Tom Gate was a real sport and I wish to place on record my sincere gratitude to him. He let me do what I wanted. Of course putting on the brake, when I was about to do anything a bit 'young'.

The net result was that in two years I built up quite a satisfactory little business. The experience I gathered was invaluable and unforgettable. One of the chief things I learnt was how to take stock of a man, and acquire a broader aspect of life.

I would also like to place on record that I became very interested in Christian Science. It helped me tremendously. Dad's position in Leicester improved, and is there on a three years contract, so, in January 1930, the family removes to Leicester, and the fickle goddess of fortune seems to have smiled on us at last. I make my home with Grannie and Ogre at Woodbottom. And I'm not sorry to have said good-bye to those unhappy years at "Hill Rise".

The summer of 1930 passes pleasantly into Autumn, and with the Autumn my tale is nearly told.

In October I come of age 'midst a positive blaze of celebration'. Good luck, and good wishes, and what is more important, ripping presents, and startling cheques seem to have poured in from every expected, and many an unexpected quarter, I feel superbly happy. Everywhere I go my health is toasted in champagne. And as Duncan and I are twins to within a week, we entertain forty-six of our friends at The Grand in Harrogate. The rich red flowed freely indeed. It was a grand show. We certainly know how to throw a party!

Incidentally, my prowess in the rugger field is mentioned in the local sporting press, and the elation of seeing ones name in print for the first time. I must curb, or I shall be wandering off into superlatives, and that would never do.

There is just one sad reflection, the National Provincial Bank have become richer by some £300 - being my Insurance that by rights should have come to me. Dad had to hand them over along with all the family holdings, as security to the Bank for Newlay.

So, I come to the end of it. And at the end of it all there are many things that I've not done yet; seen a first class Soccer match, shaved with a cut-throat razor, slept with a prostitute, looped the loop, or even seen our King or Queen in person.

After which... we come to the future, and which I shall discreetly leave to take care of itself.

After which.

Goodbye to all that...

====
====
====
====
====

I have decided to keep a diary. It ought to be rather fun really, because it won't be an ordinary sort of diary - of the New Year resolution brigade, at all. I shall only enter what I like, and when I like. That's much the best way to keep a diary - and I shall not put down the weather, unless, as tonight its really noticeable. Its cold, hellish cold. So, I suppose I've broken my first rule. But I shall not have any rules in my diary. I shall be free in it, to write what I please -

Free; Ah-ha, that sounds good.

October,1930.

News in chunks - in very great chunks. I have only started to keep a Diary, and I am breaking my first rule!

I have been offered an excellent opportunity, that of working for Mr. Richard Nickols, Burley Mills, Leeds, and at nearly double the salary I am getting now.

I have had a long chat with Mr. Gate, and his advice is that I must not miss it - so here goes.

November 11th, 1930.

I have been at Burley Mills for just a week. The whole concern is best described as one large happy family. At least I think so at present. I wont bother you with personalities. But I like every one of them. They all show individuality and character. If I just stick to my work and concentrate on the job on hand, and when I go travelling; bring back a few orders. Put my back into it; as I intend. I shall gee.

The present arrangement is for me to have about 6 months in the Kip Warehouse, Works, and dressed Warehouse - then to start travelling. I wonder how much wiser of the world I shall be by November 11th, 1931.

Which brings me to a very solid sort of thought... that at the age of twenty one I am entirely self-supporting, and what counts for more is that I lead a normal civilised existence in as much as I have a good time, please myself and enjoy myself tremendously. I have a few damn fine pals and a whole heap of acquaintances.

I drink a silent toast.

November 29th, 1930.

To quote Pooh Bear, I have today, thought "A Very Great Thought." I think I am growing up, or at least I think so, because the less I see of Bill, Lewis and Duncan, the less I feel that high-sounding thing called romantic friendship, but which I prefer to call hero worship. A friendship with no other physical attraction than a good friendly scrap, which for me constitutes some of the manliest pleasures attainable. Of course there are other ways of getting pleasures - the sheer physical joy out of a long walk or a hard swim.

I like cleanliness, straightforwardness, health and beauty. I am content.

Old Year's Night, or New Year's Eve, or December 31st 1930.

Looking back on the past year. It has been (as usual) one of noble endeavour - frequently frustrated, but invariably well meant. In accordance with the custom of the newspapers, I am setting down its record of achievements in various callings, and I offer the public in full confidence of its sympathy and appreciation.

Games: Made good progress with the Ball Game, and was actually mentioned in the local sporting press, but then slacked off horribly. Marbles, satisfactory, whilst Ner and Spell (in a dark corner) have made rapid strides. Billiards digress - I mean the opposite to progress. On the whole it has been a year of general satisfaction.

Finance: The old system of keeping no accounts and never filling in the counterfoils has again answered admirably.

Pets: Ezikiel, the cat, perished in May. The Doctor said it was too much exercise on an empty... Well, he put it rather crudely. You know how cats will exercise. Altogether a bad year for pets.

Thought: As usual, little thinking has been accomplished. It has been a year of very little thought. As the Duchess said to Alice "....- Never imagine yourself not to be otherwise, than what you might appear to others than that what you were, or might have been not otherwise than what you had been, would you have appeared to them to be otherwise!

Xylonite: *[Xylonite was brand-name for an early type of plastic. Fibrous vegetable matter (e.g. cotton and flax waste and old rags), dissolved in acid and neutralised, which produced a substance called Parkesine, named after its inventor, Edmund Alexander Parkes (1813–90), of Birmingham. In its liquid state it was used as a waterproofing agent and in its plastic form for insulation]* I have not done any of this.

Wisdom lingers: At the end of it I can truthfully say that I am if not a year wiser - a year fatter, and a year older - Oh, yes, I was forgetting. I am 21. I am a man.

I wonder?

January 3rd, 1931.

Living at Lee House:
I, somehow cannot understand it. I have been so ridiculously happy in spasms. I wont even attempt to describe them. It would only spoil their beauty. Perhaps it is because I am living away from home, and finding my feet, as the saying is; perhaps it is the counter-action of Monday when everything went wrong, as things have a wretched habit of doing. I lost my temper with every-body and everything. But worse than that, it was a complete breakdown of my mental make-up. I failed to master myself at rather a critical time. It was a pi period, whatever that may mean.

On Saturday, I went to Duncan's. It was hellish foggy. And so we bridged for about four and a half hours, then settled down to listen to Ambrose's band till midnight, finishing off the evening with a good old fight.

Byway of a contrast, Sunday was a typical winters day - clear and frosty, yet strangely warm in the winters sun. The four of us went for a good long walk in the afternoon, and back to a tea of hot buttered muffins. Then evening, sitting round the cosy fireside, in the twilight of a red and glowing fire - tinged with purple frosty flames. Easy chairs, the gramophone, the comfy feel of old clothes, and the happy touch of friendly fingers. Its all rather glorious, you know.

I walked back to Lee House over the Hunger Hills, by the Church, and behind the old Hall. The moon was full and of exceptional brilliance, and even though the sky was clear there was not a star to be seen. I cannot describe either the shade of blue or the look of the trees in the silvery moonshine. The tranquillity of it all. I felt a very warm glow.

January 12th, 1931.

This evening I have just realised, perhaps more fully than before that between Betty and myself there is no physical element in our friendship. But then that applies to all my friendships so far.

What is Love?

I suppose love is a subject, of which every young man thinks he knows something, and, therefore it is rather banal to discuss it. Incidentally it is one of those subjects about which most of them know nothing, and so it's equally useless. I suppose, to the majority of young men it is the curiosity of suppressed sex. To me, I hold "Love" on a very different plane of thought.

I think a suitable epitaph for me would be :-

What I aspired to be,
And was not, comforts me.

With apologies, to whoever bothers to claim them.

January 17th, 1931.

A terrible thing happens, and in consequence, I learn A Very Big Lesson... namely keep myself to myself.

February 1st, 1931.

Today much has happened.

In the morning I had intended to go to Church, but, on awaking found two inches of snow - so I stayed in and cleaned my Rugger Boots, then finished off with a snow fight with Michael in the Garden. But it is thawing fast.

Had a very excellent dinner. Aunt Jane's always are.

Duncan calls as usual in his old "Iron Horse". We had not been at Fence End more than a few minutes when Bill accidentally clocked me one on the nose, which proceeded to bleed like holy hell. During our customary and time-honoured walk, in which the usual rowdism took place, for instance I was lucky enough to plant Lewis, most beautifully, in a holly bush, but he was soon to have his revenge; for when passing the mill, he picked me bodily up and dropped me into a pond of melted snow. The others say it was damn funny. It is always easy to laugh at the adversity of others.

They say it ought to be the seventh funniest thing. (The others being:-

The Dust fight between Bill and Lewis.

My being stripped on the tennis lawn at "Fence-End".

Boating, or rather learning to use a punt at Wetherby, and going round in circles.

By Bottle Party, at "Woodbottom",

Bill's Bottle Party, at "The Hawthorns".

The fun at Bramley Baths.)

I am, however, in entire disagreement. I assure you it is highly uncomfortable with your pants sticking to your skin - to say nothing of your trousers.

Duncan lends me some clothes, and we have tea. After which I discover a quality in my self that I was none too sure I possessed. It happened like this:

I wanted the easy-chair, and Lewis - Silent Wolf, wanted the same. I was there first... I will leave it to your imagination as to what followed, but if you have never had the good fortune to be in the Billiards Rooms round about 5.30 on a Sunday afternoon-cum-evening, you will not have the remotest. Civilisation loses all hold on us. We become barbarians. On we went for over 40 minutes, though neither of us won, by that I mean neither of us had the chair for more than a moment or two, and, neither of us being British, would give way. So; it is demonstrated that even a child might lead me, but even dear old Lewis cannot drive me... to quote Bill.

Strewth! I was as stubborn as a mule. God knows how I stuck it. I was done after the first few minutes. The fight finished in a somewhat dramatic finale. We both had the chair, and shook hands right heartily on it, and to me, that alone, was worth it.

I know I was very nearly out (I've only felt like that once before). Its hard to describe, a lump comes in your throat, if you do not keep talking to someone, or keep a very firm hold on yourself. I should have simply broken down and blubbered, and that would never do for a fellow of 21.

February 27th, 1931.

I must review the events of this week with certain amount of misgiving. Much water has flowed beneath the bridges, and much ale has passed the portals.

On Tuesday, The Bohemians had their Annual Hot Pot at "The Guilford" in Leeds. King Belly, bless his holy name. I decorated my inside in a manner that is unbecoming to a gentleman. The net result is that I have resolved not to drink beer again.On Wednesday, The Burley Mills Sports Club hold their Annual Dance at The Railway Mens Club in Hunslet. Ye Gods, if only I were humorously inclined, it would be uproarious. It is an absolutely filthy working mens club, situated in a district to tone, one that is hardly noted for its cleanliness, being the only representative of the staff, I was left with the baby to hold - give the prizes, et cetera. When dancing with a girl in the Paul Jones, I made the observation that the room was getting a little thick, and I was completely flattened with her reply "...Yes! I am just starting to get all sweaty now." But in spite of it all I quite enjoyed it. For a decorative scheme - some cheap artist had decorated the walls in the French Renaissance style. Romeos and Juliets in lurid pinks and purples, walking in a poor, but highly imaginative imitation of the Tuileries *[formal gardens next to the Louvre in Paris. The gardens are all that remain of the Tuileries Palace, a royal residence begun in 1564 and burnt down in 1871 during the Commune of Paris.]*, complete with peacocks and naked babies. The result was too idiotic for words.

One thing, however, about being a member of the Working Mens Club (and I was made one for the evening), you can get bitter beer - inflicted for some obscure reason with the name of "omie".   I was given to understand that it had been brewed by the Affiliated Clubs Union Brewery. It costs only 5d a pint, whilst a small whiskey and splash runs you to 7d. I give these figures for comparative purposes.

On Thursday evening, I did a little Boxing at the Gym at Burley Mills, and enjoyed it immensely. Mike Sunderland, one of the workmen, runs the show. He is an amusing character, one of the old hard-bitten school. Coming from a fighting stock, he lives and thinks as a fighter should - though God knows how that is!

Saw Lewis on Friday Evening, and he is of the opinion that if a fellow gets a decent girl, with really decent ideals it will help him immensely in his work and life generally. Lew tells me plainly that he would think more of me if I...

March 7th 1931.

On my first visit to The Opera, or, As you like it. I fear my education must have been sadly neglected in infancy for I am over twenty-one before I see my first Opera. But then my parents have never displayed any literary or artistic leanings of any description.

The curtain goes up: what then, it might have been Musical Comedy. I saw the Gondoliers. If I may criticise, I would say they sang too much. If you are a little fagged - or jaded, it is rather a marvellous restive. "...of that there is no shadow of doubt, all probable possible shadow of doubt, all possible doubt whatever..."

March 17th 1931.

It is funny; when life goes well, how pleasant it can be. When it is the end of the month, and you are to draw close upon £17, and you have been lucky to bring home a few good orders, and when you are feeling in the pink of condition. Yea, verily, *Le Joie de vivre!*... Then sometimes when things don't just go your way - it is surprising how soon you can lose your patience, and interest, and humour in life. And you come to experience that sort of bottomless feeling.

I've gone and bought a car for really far more than I can afford. I expect I shall get horribly ticked off at home. But I had to make up my mind right away. You know I rather miss Mum and Dad in such moments, when I have to make immediate decisions. But after all... it is, as Browning says, 'Character is made by the way we take trouble. Character is the greatest thing in the world, greater than anything. Its a really big thing character is.'

What does anything matter so long as we don't cry out, when we're hurt, or give in when were beaten to our knees.

Saturday, May 16th 1931.

In a diary, I suppose it is generally (subconsciously or not), the thing to relate the events which have a happy memory, or, on the other hand the reverse. But today has been one of the former type. First we (Duncan and I) went Rook Shooting at Hawkesworth Hall, and had some excellent sport, bringing to earth some thirty birds. This was followed by three pretty strenuous sets of tennis at Fence-End. And not being satisfied, we went up to Bramley for a good hard swim. We spent the first part of the evening doing what lots of young chaps are wont to do [For the life of me I cannot remember now (i.e Summer 1926) who it was. Was it Dot and Olga, Pearl and Hilda, or Eyes and Winnie, or Laura and Edith, or Peggy, or Dorothy Smith, or "Tret-me-rough" and Connie or even Rose and Ann. We did have some amusing evenings, I shall never forget the evening when Bill Irwin first came to Horsforth, going out with Rose and Ann to the old Dutch Barn behind the old Hall, and getting caught by a Bobbie. It is all very delightful now, but at that moment we didn't think so.]

it was all very happy and peaceful - in the woods at Leathley, complete with gramophone. We finished the evening by listening to Ambrose until midnight. I felt very happy. To quote my contemporary "...and with more enjoyment, and so to bed".

The following day I shall always remember vividly enough, half a dozen words are ample.

"Rose and Ann in Eccup Woods".

Sunday, May 31st, 1931.

This morning I went to Mick's Boxing Show at Burley Mills and was lucky enough to see some very fair sport. Isn't it strange, how many of us would rather go to a boxing show than praise the Lord on a Sunday morning?

It is either a case of that men fail to get any uplift from religion, which means that religion has failed; but perhaps the mentality of man retarded. I am sure this modern trend against religion is having a very bad effect on us - as a community at large. I think it is already very much in evidence, becoming much more so since the war. The whole thing is very complicated.

Then the little things; (of course, in reality they are very big things) but it is amazing how indifferent we have become, I might almost say bored with such things as trains, babies, immorality, wireless and The Empire. And the way we get our amusements literally rammed down our throats. Ha-ha, my friend, the perils of commercialism. I am sure we were much better citizens, when we were made to make our own amusements, which incidentally tended to become productive. God bless the memory of Queen Victoria!

To revert to our muttons. We went boating at Wetherby in the afternoon. It's no use, I didn't enjoy it a little bit. Anne didn't turn up, and the midges were hell. It rained. The punting... well, that's enough.

Some Confessions.

What makes life worth living?
A clean mentality, that urges men to do finer things.

What is the most lovable quality in the human being for whom you have the most regard?
An unselfish love - and thoughtfulness.

What is the most detestable quality in anyone you dislike?
Lying.

What is the most attractive quality in yourself?
That's not fair.

...And the most detestable?
I wonder - perhaps...

What living celebrity do you admire the most?
I'm not sure, T.E. Lawrence, or Queen Mary.

What gives you the greatest pleasure?

A new book, a square meal, new clothes, or hard exercise, and a hot bath?

Ah! That's too easy.

If you were to begin your life again. What career would you choose?

The same. I wonder, if I shall always hold this view.

Undated, - sometime in June.

At Leicester. Tonight I feel bloody miserable. Mum and Dad have had a real old row. I shall never marry. Mother has such a frightful money-spending mania. But then at times she is so adorably lovely and perfectly brilliant both socially and domestically. Actually Father has no room to talk. He is damned extravagant, and the worst of it is that I have inherited it from both of them, anyway, thank God I have assured myself for quite a decent sum £400, and that is one form of saving, and at the same time a sound investment.

Stray Thoughts - undated.

...and so I find myself wondering to what will it all lead? There must be a breaking point somewhere, and we shall reach it sooner or later. When it will be necessary to abandon beliefs we now hold. Our ideals will have to be lowered. Firstly that of comfort, and that of cleanliness - never before, at any time in the history of man have these two ideals been brought to a higher pitch of excellence. An analysis of any extinct nation will show that when these two peaks have been reached... decay sets in, and their future rapidly decided. The main difference is that we have the whole world to face; we know for example what the shape of the world is; and speaking practically there are no new lands awaiting discovery. Today, even the navvy's son has a chance of a university career. Of course, on the other hand, the disease is world-wide.

What we want today is a leader - a great leader. But wither shall we look for him. We must stop drifting at all events.

It amazes me that we take our troubles in such a 'come day, go day' fashion. Some day the Country and its Empire will have to face some unpleasant realities, and of a greater seriousness than any of us ever dream.

June 12th, 1931.

News in chunks.

It is positively breath-taking. Tonight I have been informed that I am to represent the firm of Richard Nickols in Ireland - their most lucrative ground, and that I am to sail either Sunday night, or Monday morning. I do hope I can show them what I am made of. The traditional strategy of the family and all that. It is a tremendous honour and I only hope that I shall be able to justify their confidence in me.

Colin is - - - (Well, I've changed my mind, and I wont write what I think). Yes, you can put your shirt on little Archibald.

August Bank Holiday - 1931. Camping out at Filey.

A camping holiday... how can I best describe it?

In any case holidays have a very disturbing effect on the mind - sort of temporary unbalancing the equilibrium of one's thought.

The ideal holiday in my opinion is to let my will go where it will. To do what I like, just when I like, and how I like. This year Duncan and myself have really done it, and have pulled together wonderfully, it has been tremendous fun.

Camp, with its cold grey dawn, when the dew is heavy and everything is damp and cold. Camp, with its happy smell of smouldering logs. Camp, with its earwigs, beetles, and water fatigues. Camp, with its potato peeling, and washing-up of greasy pots in cold water. Camp, with its 'one-wash-a-day' feeling... and that gentle peace of mind which falls when sitting round the glowing embers of a dying fire, or when lying all tucked up in your flee bag - idly watching the reflection of the flickering flames dancing on the sides of the tent, and, faintly through the open flap - comes the drone of the incoming tide, and the gulls - their final calls. Then comes a peace - Ah, well! Today we bathed and lay on the beach for a couple of hours. It's rather marvellous, you know, to be quite
naked in the sun, with your eyes closed - doing nothing - thinking of nothing. Just letting your thoughts come as they will... Just wondering why.

Back to earth, just before I left, Mr. Clarkson, the manager at Burley Mill, called me into his office, and gave me a fiver from Mr. Richard Nickols who was extremely pleased with the report on my first visit to Ireland. Unfortunately, Mr. Richard was very poorly at home, and could not give it me in person. I felt, as you can imagine, tremendously bucked - not so much with the fiver (though it was heartily welcome), but with the thought that I had been a success in handling the largest account of the firm.

August 1st, 1931.

Mr. Richard Nickols passes on. I feel, and very deeply too, that I have lost a very good friend. He is cremated, and the remains interred at Spofforth Church.

August 16th 1931.

A Cork - Liverpool crossing on a sticky night.

What an amazing experience - so much so that I am mentioning it here. It marks a period when I am becoming a better sailor (or is it only fancy?).

A brief description of the tug, S.S. Kenmare, built in the year I was born (1909) and of a gross tonnage of just over 1,000 tons. She takes about 50 passengers, and the rest is cargo of all descriptions, including some quantities of pigs and cows and the like.

With no fuss the anchor is drawn, and we start. For the first two or three hours it is all very wonderful going down the harbour to Queenstown - then out into the open Atlantic - that is a real thrill, quite definitely. Shortly afterwards, the smoke room loses one of its company, and I retire very early to bed, as I deem it wiser to be horizontal, than vertical, when the old tub begins her antics.

The "Kenmare" has only two State rooms; in other words can have the doubtful pleasure of sleeping therein. It is really great fun trying to undress when there's a heavy sea running. You endeavour to put your collar on what you think is a shelf, and find that it has found a home in the wash basin.

Outside my cabin (and mine is next to the captain's on the bridge) great excitement prevails - whistles keep getting blown, and bells occasionally rung, and some bright individual is violently sick outside my cabin. About ten p.m. (I forget how many bells), the cows and the rest of the live-stock set off a deuce of a shindy, and the engines keep on throbbing. But still it's great fun. Oh, Lord, as I am trying to write this, the individual outside is off again. It is some consolation to know that he or she cannot possibly keep it up all night.

Dawn, at last - how wonderful it really is. I wouldn't have realised how appreciable it is to be able to stretch your legs and fill your lungs with the bracing cool sea air, and to feel gently warmed by the golden glow in the eastern sky. Then comes the sun, what a vivid contrast to the clear blue sky, which is dotted just here and there with pale feathered clouds. I lean against the railings, and watch the brilliant sun dance and sparkle over the sea towards me. Its magnificence is nearly blinding. Turning away, the sea looks very cold and merciless, in its old grey-blue coat.

The Mersey at last. It will be good to feel the land again after a tossing of 22 hours.

August 17th, 1931.

Oh! My comrade! Bill, I've not much sympathy for you. You have learnt your lesson, very sorely, and with considerable bodily harm I fear. There was a time, and not so long ago, when I put Lewis before everything and everybody. But I learned my lesson, and I now look upon him a little more as myself and not so much of a god. One thing I learned, that to give way to his bidding, as Bill evidently did is only asking for trouble. I am sure Lewis likes a chap better for sticking up to him. If Duncan ever sees this, he will say I'm a fibber - He says, "you're always so weak, if Lewis ever suggests anything, you always agree".

Bill failed at the water jump. It was an acid test to any friendship. When four have to live, sleep and eat at so close a range, a small boat on the Broads and it rains day after day - one is apt (and does) get a bit edgy. But its none of my business, so I'll say no more.

September 30th, 1931.

The Heavy Gang (Duncan, Bill, Lewis and Self), that infallible institution, is disintegrating.

The last of the Corinthians.

Even Pug and myself are fading.

Its tragic.

Why should women be allowed to interfere with so sacred a friendship.

October 1st 1931.

Damn! Everything has gone wrong today.
I have made several bad slips at Burley.

The Biggest Show Ever.

I have a life to live - another 50 years or so (D.V.) *[the Latin words: Deo Volente – meaning, "God willing."]*
Only once can I live it. What is the most good to which I can put it? What is the noblest object to live for?
Paul tells us without a moments hesitation it is love. John goes one further and says, "God is Love" - as it is the Law which fills the Ten Commandments. Let us analyse LOVE:-

Patience: This is the normal attitude of love - waiting to begin; Love not in a hurry; calm.

Kindness: Love active efficient, making people happy, in doing good turns.

Generosity: Lose NO chance in giving pleasure.

Eliminate the spirit of ill-will and thought.

Humility: Love hides even from itself.

Courtesy: This is love in society - in relation to our general bearing.

Unselfishness: The difficult thing, is to give up ourselves.

But it is more difficult not to seek things for ourselves - well - seek them not.

There is no greatness in things, because they will crumble. Nothing is a hardship to love. Half the world is on the wrong scent, in their hunt for happiness. They think it consists of having and getting and being served.

Good Temper: Isn't this remarkable? Love is not easily provoked. There are two classes of sins - of the body, and of disposition.   Society does not hesitate as to which is the worse.   But are we right? We have no balance in which to weigh one another's sins... as to which are the finer and coarser. Good temper is the test of love - anything that is unchristian is all symbolised on one little flash of temper.

Guilelessness and sincerity: The possession of these are the great secret of personal influence. It is wonderful in this hard world to be an optimist - a man that puts the best construction on every action.

What is the secret of success? What makes a brilliant sprinter, boxer, swimmer, shot or bridge player?... Only practice - and nothing else. Life is not a holiday, but an education; and so we get dozens of opportunities to practice in the stream of life: Goethe says:

"Talent develops in solitude;
Character in the stream of life."

Love itself can never be defined. It is most certainly not a thing of enthusiastic emotion. Love as a religion comes not by chance, but by a natural or super-natural law... so says Dr Henry Drummond in his essay. It was Dr. Cove-Smith - an old Rugby International - who said... "Christ was a real out-of-doors man, muscular, and no milk sop. He was a born skipper of a team.

October 29th, 1931.

Bengal Lancer - F.Yates Brown, - Polo, *[This book was first published in 1930. Written by a British officer between 1905 and 1925, Francis Yates-Brown witnessed the Indian army's development from an old-style frontier and garrison army to one that was forced to deal with the modern rigours of a World War. The book includes...]*
Picksticking - Soldering - Mysticism.

November 15th, 1931.

On my third business trip to Ireland I met with several biographical details worthy of record. The first was my performing the acrobatic feat of kissing the blarney stone. It is strange how small heights of a couple of hundred feet or so make me feel quite giddy. My second was a visit to Messrs. Guinness Brewery - what a warming thought. They brew some 2,000,000 gallons of porter and Stout a week. I was amazed to learn how they have dispensed with unnecessary labour and pumping. The liquor all flows by gravitation. Another thing that interested me was the tradition in the cooperage department, that it is a hereditary job. The sons serving their apprenticeship, not to the firm as might be generally supposed, but to their Fathers or Uncles. Of course, I can readily understand that a 'barrel-smellers' job is highly skilled - what a calamity if he caught cold, because he's on 'piece work' rate of pay!

Ireland, in general, is just what I expected - invariably there is a background of mountains, and a foreground of marshy waste, intermingled with rocks, and generally there is a lake not far away, which makes a sharp and happy contrast. Honestly, I don't know how some of the Irish in the west country manage to exist at all. The squalor and filth is nauseating, but I suppose it all fits into the order of things. I think the smell of their peat fires is very attractive.

November 20th, 1931. I Visit "Genesis".

When I saw Mr. Epstein's "Genesis", I can honestly say that I felt an inclination to take off my hat. It really is most extraordinary. Many people say that it is vile. But its curves curiously arrest one's attention. Men will long debate as to its theory, and what was at the back of Mr. Epstein's mind when he sculptured it. *[Jacob Epstein's 'Genesis' shows a woman in the late stages of pregnancy. It is carved out of marble and is extremely heavy (almost 3 tonnes). It was first exhibited at Bluecoat, Liverpool in 1931 when nearly 50,000 visitors paid sixpence (about £2.50 in today's money) to see what was considered Britain's most shocking sculpture. It was brought to Bluecoat to raise money to help fund the building. 86 years later, Genesis returned to Bluecoat during the building's 300th anniversary year in 2017. In 1931, the sculpture divided opinion. Some people thought it was beautiful and others that it was shocking, ugly and not even art. The artist regarded his sculpture as very calm and peaceful.]*

Post Script. I learn that The Leeds Corporation intend to buy the statue, and to have it erected in City Square as a memorial to the women who fell in the Great War 1914-1918.

January 1932

Sycamore Square

Sycamore Square is quiet and small
In shape it isn't
    A Square at all.
Its long and narrow
    And a Cul-de-Sac,
When you want to get out,
    You've to go to the back.
But everybody -
    Thats ever been there,
Tries to settle for ever
    In Sycamore Square.
Its houses are white,
    and its railings are green,
Its garden is tidy,
    and tiny and clean.
(For there's no room for -
    anyone
In it you see
    Save for the fish in the fountain

The birds in the trees
    The cats on the flagstones,
The sun and the rain
    And William the gardener -
(Just now and again).
    Oh, Everybody
That's ever been there
    say there's no place -
In London,
    Like Sycamore Square.

    To   Betty
    "The White House"
    Belgrave   Road
    Barnes. London S.W.

    O, Lord, I suppose I must be in love!

February 4th, 1932.

This week, I seem to have spent most of my time travelling in trains over the hills and dales of bonnie Scotland; but the time slipped quickly away. I had plenty of good books.

To me, there is a great joy in spooning soup or hacking at a chop; while the scenery of mother England is being swiftly unrolled on either side; in rushing through several hundred yards of space between one bite and the next. I appreciate with feeling that anyone who dines on a train has cunningly killed time, having cheated the journey out of its monotonous hours.

At last we arrive in Edinburgh - that wonderful city. Today I visited the War Memorial, which is, perhaps, one of the most outstanding monuments of its kind in the country. In the shrine we can remember our brothers and cousins who fought and died not only for us, but their Empire, in decency and quietness.

February 7th, 1932. Wondering Why!

Do you ever go there?
To the great city of thought?
Memory, Wonderment, Melancholy... and the rest. I am rather fond of going there and wandering through its broad silent streets. There are three great divisions in this city... Past, Present, and Future. I wonder which is the greatest?

Aldous Huxley.

Excessive or exclusive devotion to any particular thing is bad. For instance our great mechanical progress has hindered our intellectual progress, and had hindered our emotional development. Fancy a man incapable of friendship, love and fatherhood, and the many other desirable things of life. Man should cultivate a Balance and Harmony amongst his powers; he should not sacrifice any of his instincts and desires to others.

At present, everyone is living in an age of terrific boredom. Sometime there will be a revolt, and it will be due to the fact that everyone is so terribly passive nowadays.

Very few create their own amusements. We all seem to endure and suffer them.

The funny part is, the more things we acquire, the less satisfaction they give us. Half the things we get, is not because we really want them, but because they are rammed down our throats by advertisement.

Another amazing fact of this age is the craving of everyone for a newspaper celebrity. It is not as though one took those repudiations seriously. There is an overwhelming desire to see our names in print, and in the papers. Its all very strange.

February 11th, 1932.

Have written to Betty tonight. I wonder if she keeps my letters? A big change has recently come over her letters to me. For instance the very mundane 'Dear' has now been substituted by 'My dearest'" which is distinctly more interesting.

Rugger Rhymes.

Beginning as half in the "C" XV
I appeared in the "B" and then in the "A"
And once had a gallop with THE XV,
But signally failed to stay.
I figured as 'three' in the 1st XV
As a substitute - never again;
And I was the cause of pain.

"You haven't, old fellow, the pace" they said;

"You're better at the back in the 'A'"
"Thats your natural place" they said.
And there I perform today.

I've never emerged as a three again,
But the 'A' is a haven for me,
Till I must go down to the "C" again -
By way of the loathly "B".

Acknowledgements to "Punch".

A Pinch of Salt   Robert Graves

When a dream is born within you
With a sudden clamorous pain,
When you know that dream is true
And lovely with no flaw nor stain,
Oh then, be careful, or with sudden clutch
You'll hurt the delicate thing you prize so much.

Dreams are like a bird that mocks,
Flirting the feathers of his tail
When you seize for the salt box
Over the hedge you'll see him sail
Old birds are caught with neither salt nor chaff;
They watch you from the apple bough and laugh.

Poet, never chase the dream.
Laugh yourself and turn away
Mask your hunger, let it seem
Small matter if he come or stay;

But when he nestles in your hand at last,
Close up your fingers tight, and hold him fast.

May 1932.   "Farewell"

...Since starting "The Bran Tub" - my notebook, nearly two years ago, my thoughts have altered tremendously and, I hope to some degree advanced. On reading it over, i.e. From October 1930 to February 1932, it is really a pretty poor effort, but it has served its purpose, and so there let it remain on the bottom shelf on the extreme left. *['The Bran Tub' was a handwritten notebook containing remarks and ideas that were eventually condensed into this book.]*

It is like the primroses and bluebells in June. They wither fast and soon will be lost. "The Bran Tub", withers also, it deserves no better fate. Though let me hope that foundation has been laid to some greater effort. I dare not even forecast the shape it will eventually emerge. Old David said in the Psalms "that a way will be shown".

Two years ago - I was none too sure of my ambitions. Now they are shaping, one is to hunt, if possible own a horse, and live an open-air life. Another is to be an Ambassador of clean clear thought, and to represent straight forward and honest business methods - as applied to the Leather trade. When I am double my present age, I may fancy my chances as a politician, and rise like a bubble in the sparkling water. But then political water can hardly be called clear or scintillating, can it?

Anyway the whole idea - as you may have guessed is to try hard and leave the world a little better place for my having been on it for a short while. And if I do this, I shall have achieved no small thing.

— — — — — — — —-

This last entry was the last in my note or scrap book, which I called "The Bran Tub".

About the last thirty pages have been copied, verbatim, from it.

Now comes my diary proper.

— — — — — — — —-

February 26th, 1932.

One of the objects of these odd notes is to record my thoughts, reactions, and doings at the giddy and irresponsible age of 22.

Inwardly, there is a constant change going on. I would like to analyse it, but cannot. On my way to Church this evening (in Minor [his car]), I had a shot.

Just twelve months ago, I went to the same service, but by tram and bus, and when I went I was happier and easier in my mind. Now why was that?

Since then I have got nearly everything that a young fellow can want to make life more liveable.

In the smoke room (my room) at Woodbottom - where I am surrounded by the material outcome of my thoughts and labours. Sometimes I sit and think. Sometimes I just sit. A sense of security comes over me. I may drink mine own health in my best pale sherry. Yet with all this, I am no happier. A remedy must be speedily found. There is little doubt as to where my biggest battle lies... that is,... my own soul. Nothing is impossible to the man who can direct and control this thought and imagination.

For twelve months I have carried on an intensive campaign of commercial travelling. I have been away from home almost every week, excepting for holiday times. I have covered (I might almost say combed), the Midlands, Scotland, Lancashire and Ireland, and a single journey to Bristol. It is possible that my mental unbalance from which I am now suffering is the direct result of staying in hotels for about five nights out of the seven. Hotel life, with its noisy glamour, has an appeal all on its own, and one's own fireside is the antithesis, with the result that I soon grow irritable with "Woodbottom". The fault certainly does not lie with my dear grandparents. They do everything imaginable for my comfort and general wellbeing. The household revolves round my whims. Dear old Ogre *[Tim's Grandad]*, never for one moment stops chattering and worrying when I am at home... what we shall have for breakfast luncheon, tea and dinner, and what time am I to be expected. To read a book or listen to the wireless while he's about is next door to an impossibility. You see - when I stay at the Hotel Magnificent, and something is not just to my liking, I ring a bell, and lo! It is as I want. If the chef overcooks my steak, or does not burst my sausage; back they go.

Such behaviour at home is of course absolutely taboo.

Another thing that gives cause for anxiety, in a mind way is the financial aspect; can I ever save ? Here I am with a car, once new, but now nearing old age, and I have something under ten quid towards a new one. It has been one of my long cherished ambitions to buy some aviation share.

Imperial Airways at 19/6 (£1) *[Eventually became British Airways]*
or, Faireys   at 14/9 (10/-) *[Defunct 1965]*
or, Handley Page   at 10/8 (8/- 10% Pref) *[Defunct 1970]*
or, De havillands   at 30/- (£1) *[Defunct 1963]*

I am confident that they would be a good buy. But I ask you how is this good thing to come to pass?

The Ides of March.   March 13th 1932.

A curious position has arisen. I'm worked up so to speak. Ever since I left school and endeavoured to use my mind, I've always had bags to do - always a struggle to get through my self imposed tasks: "The Bran Tub", my two note-books on Leather Manufacture, The University Leather classes, My Aviation Notes, my Stamps, and the model D.H. Moth, and always a hefty pile of letters to wade through. Many things yet remain: French, Shorthand, Accountancy, Reading (unending), and a revision of all my notes. Turning to the material since I want a portable wireless for the car and garden, and since I have taken over the furnishing of the smoke room I want a really good easy chair. This embraces such financial outlay that I cannot bring my plans to fruition as yet. I'm optimistic. It will come one day.

It's really wonderful to have such fine fellows as Bill, Lewis and Duncan for pals. And what a difference a cheery spring-like day makes on us all. Our wits are perceptibly sharpened. It is good to have a Sunday afternoon together again. It is the first time for about a month that us lads have had a Heavy Gang Sunday altogether again. Lewis is too busy with his Rugger, lakin' *[playing]* (as they say in Yorkshire) for his County, and next year I hope it will be his Country, and courting. Duncan is too busy with his girlfriends, he was bragging the other day that he had been out ten evenings running and had had a different each evening... Ye Gods! And Bill is too busy making his fortune. There is nobody so much respected in this world as a stingy rich man. But I don't think Bill will be stingy. This afternoon we were all in ripping form, *qui n'a sante, n'a rien*, (He that has not good health has nothing..) After we had had our usual coffee at The Hawthorns, we played an impromptu game of soccer, then hockey (two aside) in Mathers field - until we were told to clear off, and I had my trousers ripped off - such brutality! In the early evening we played snooker, and played the fool generally at The Barret Mansions. Enjoyed ourselves to the hilt - so what matters?

What a difference it makes to life when you are surrounded by three healthy young fellows - who are anything but snobs, or anything gutless. Their influence has advanced my ability (what little I have) -- tremendously. Lewis fills me with noble ideals, he's as hard as nails. Bill spurns me on to greater things in life. And Duncan - God knows what, he's magnificent!

After tea, this afternoon, we sat in the billiard room and debated as to whether the tennis lawn should be turned into a Rose garden. Or are we to take up the game seriously? If not, the game will lose two master strokes...

"The swan-neck lob", and 'The bucket shop'. These two strokes have undoubtedly put the second 'n' in Tennis.

March 14th, 1932.

Pressed.

Pressed out of measure
    and pressed to all length,
Pressed so intensely
    it seems beyond strength.
Pressed in the body
    and Pressed in the soul,
Pressed in the mind
    till the dark surges roll.
Pressure by foes, and
    pressure from friends,
Pressure and pressure -
    till life nearly ends.
Pressed into knowing
    no helper but God,
Pressed into loving
    the staff and the rod,
Pressed into liberty
    where nothing clings,
Pressed into faith
    for impossible things
Pressed into living
    a life in the Lord
Pressed into living -
    A Christ-Life outpoured.

March 15th, 1932.

Lewis tells me that I must make up my mind about Betty. To what extent do I love her? He says it will be fatal to take up the sympathetic attitude now that they have lost their brass. Goodbye to Pool Hall, goodbye the peacocks, goodbye the pigeons. *Sic transit gloria mundi.* Either I love Betty for loves sake, or I don't: Which? I'm blessed if I know. The logical conclusion to the argument is - "Will you become my wife?" the contemplation of which is rather devastating. Now that she has gone to London, carrying on one's courtship by postal instalments is somewhat complicated. When we do meet, its only for a short time and we are both on our best behaviour, in consequence neither of us know of what the other is made. I admit that a good wife can literally 'make' her man. I have a feeling that I should go a long way in this world if I were pushed by the right girl. Someone in whom I could confide, without fear of ridicule, with those every-day trivialities, and there are so many.

It's so difficult living at Woodbottom, old Ogre just descends on you, he wants to know this, that and the other - never a moment's breather.

Last night I went out with Dorothy (Smith). She is a sweet kid. In the afternoon she came down to witness my efforts on the rugger fields, and I call that damned sporting. I wonder would Betty do that for me, and be really intelligently interested? Actually I think she is rather too "refeened" (!) for the mud and blood of a rugger field.

Dorothy said she'd heard a rumour that I was engaged to a girl in London.   What-ho, Mrs. Grundy.

March 26th, 1932. Easter.

God! What an Easter.
May its memories never fade.
Today has been filled with many blessings. I see for the first time the glories of the English Lakes, and I lose 10/- in as many minutes at Pontoon *[a card game]*, and decide that it is a good thing - just now and again to go on the bust.

We had a pretty lousy train journey up to Keswick (our headquarters), which necessitated no less than four changes. Bill, the silly ass, went and pushed his fist through a railway carriage window at Lancaster, but was luckily little the worse. And we had a glorious melee with the electric light bulbs.

The Lakes at last. There are bug hunters of all types; ambitious maidens, with camp-stool, and drawing board. There are those that rise with the sun or before, and those that don khaki shorts, and grasp stout sticks, and leave the ground floor, long before the more leisured class have had their morning tea... these stay on the water level, and sail boats - play clock golf - and sup their evening coffee on neat lawns on the lakeside complete in evening dress.

What a thrill I get out of a keen game of Rugger, though I never appreciated the fact at Wrekin. It is really wonderful to be matched against such clean white chaps as either the Keswick or Cockermouth fifteens. They were in magnificent trim; this makes me a trifle ashamed of my own physical fitness - by comparison. Damn my eyesight!

Today's match has been made more memorable by the amazing scenic beauty of the field's position. It is completely hemmed in by mountains, and at the same time overlooking Derwentwater. Ideal spring-like weather prevails, together with just the right mixture of sun and cloud to develop the landscape; some of the mountains basking in the warmth of the former, and the others hiding in the shadow the latter... I was feeling surprisingly clear headed, and alert. That invigorating freshness of the air, and the delicate outline of the mountains.

The spectators - some two hundred men and their women folk, belonged to that traditional Cumberland type; that hard clean, healthy, enthusiastic and appreciative type; that make Rugger a better game for their support.

The gentle smell of the briar, and cigar, and earth, mingle with the crisp air wafting across the field in the pleasant breeze is very bracing. *La joie de vivre.*

A hot bath - a cold shower - a mug of ale - another mug of ale - a bright fire - a comfy chair - some comfy shoes - a pipe - I feel a bit stiff; but pleasantly so, and very content. Tonight, later on, after dinner we shall all get gloriously druffen.

27:3:32

We did.

28:3:32

We did again.

31:3:32

The best holiday ever. The great thing about a holiday, is that there is always another to look forward to, and, it is in the intelligent anticipation that we get our most pleasurable moments. Happy is the man that can return to work from his holiday with the same zest in which he sets off.

April 20th, 1932. A visit to The Wedgewood Pottery.

Today, I have visited the famous 'Wedgewood' Pottery factory at Etruria, Newcastle-under-Lyme. It was exceedingly interesting. For the semi-technical: we learn that earthenware pottery is made from a mixture of China clay, French clay, and Ball clay, and also calcined flint.

China or Porcelain (Translucent Ware) is made from the same mixture, but with Ball Clay omitted, and Ox-bone ash substituted in its stead. This gives the characteristic translucent effect.

The mixture is very finely ground, by somewhat primitive methods, then the white clay is forced through a series of super-fine sieves. Water is the diluent, which is later pressed out in strong canvas bags, so fine indeed, that the excess water is clean enough to drink. The clay is now ready for the potters bench.

One youth was remarkable; his hands so fine and soft, and his gentle control over the clay no less remarkable. I was amazed to see how they allow for contraction in the 'fires'. Some of the highly glazed and expensive china may have passed through as many as seven 'fires'. The glazing liquid is chiefly Borax.

The hand-painting room is very interesting, and it is no idle boast, that in this room we were privileged to see some of the finest examples of pottery that the world has ever seen - no previous civilisation has produced anything to compare with it.

Another department worthy of mention is that where the reliefs were being stuck on the famous 'Wedgewood', Blue, Black, or Sage green. It is all done with a little water and a lot of patience.

A remarkable feature lies in the fact that nearly 50% of the pottery is wasted in breakages. Hence the high cost of "Wedgewood Ware". They will not sell any 'seconds'.

Harold, our guide, told us that it was almost impossible to get a really perfect piece of China, in the sense of being absolutely blemish-less. The firm of Wedgewood employ nearly 600 hands, and it is interesting to note that Mr. Josiah Wedgewood founded the business in 1759, and that the firm is still carried on by his direct descendants.

[Amazingly, you can still take the same tour around Wedgewood today.]

April 28th, 1932.

A visit to the Dublin Factory of Messrs. W.D. and H.O. Wills Limited. [They also had factories in London, Bristol, Swindon, Newcastle and Glasgow, such was the scale of the tobacco industry.]

Somehow I was not too impressed with this factory. Perhaps I expected too much. I was also irritated by our guide; she was altogether too vague, graphic, and untechnical.

This branch of the Imperial Tobacco Company employs about 900 operatives, about 80 per cent of these are women. We saw, briefly :-

The tobacco leaf arrives from America in large barrels (delightfully vague), then after a very careful checking, the leaves are steamed to soften. The stalks are removed by hand; each girl having to do 80 lbs each day, but a nimble fingered girl will be able to increase this total to a hundred and twenty pounds a day, thereby earning a substantial bonus. The stalks go back to the customs people for rebate. The leaf (still in moist condition) is then chopped dried and cooled, and left for a few hours to 'come to'. We were not initiated into the mysteries of blending. Rather pointless keeping us out. The actual machine for making cigarettes is an absolute masterpiece of mechanical timing and adjustment. The machines are capable of turning out 1,030 cigarettes per minute. (One machine can actually produce 1,350). There were a battery of eight similar machines, and each one working eight and a half hours a day. There's a nice
little sum for you!

The packing machines, whilst ingenious were quite logical. We were also shown the making and rolling of Plug Tobacco *[Plug is the pressed block of tobacco that you would then run through a cutter to cut into flakes - essentially removing that last cutting step; it's uncut flake tobacco. It leaves the end-user with the option of how thick or thin they want to cut the tobacco]*, and snuff *[a fine tobacco which is not smoked but snorted]*. In the steaming process, of the pipe tobacco department, there was a distinct smell of acetic acid. My query was answered by a 'put-you-off' sort of smile from our guide.

The only other department that interested me was the making of cigarettes by hand. A clever girl can make upwards of 200 a day. She had very dextrous fingers.

Some of the machines were made in Great Britain, and the rest in America.

The visit was concluded by signing the 'Visitors Book', and our being presented with a small memento - a small tin of Cigarettes - all in quite nice taste.

Cigarette smokers in the British Isles smoke altogether about fifty thousand million cigarettes in a year.

Friday, May 13th, 1932.

Today, I have decided - for the time being at all events to keep a daily diary. It might even bring me luck, because today is notoriously unlucky.

The only thing that has happened today has been a verbal battle with Arthur Summerton, the cashier at Burley Mills. The outcome of which is that I get my car allowance raised from a 1d to 2d a mile - meaning on an average about three bob a week more to the firm, and I'll wager the miserable old Wesleyan never forgets it. In my opinion clerks, and the like invariably grow as narrow as the books they work amongst, in their outlook towards life. Summerton is under the impression that I am running the car entirely out of the firm, which of course is absurd. The whole incident cropped up after my having detailed Walter Redshaw off to clean the car last Saturday morning.

I can just imagine Arthur saying to himself "Who is he to say 'Do this' and 'Do that'" Its taught me a lesson... to always look upon Arthur and Miss Whitaker (though really I am very fond of her) with reserve.

Up to the present I have always attempted to work with the 'Senate', and treat it with a studied courtesy. And in the circumstances, whatever I have asked has not been unreasonable. All measures, ideas, and reforms have been introduced in the orthodox way. If the management are to be of any value, they must face up to their responsibilities, and be open to intelligent criticism. Perhaps I have been too previous in trying to establish myself, but I think not.

Whilst on the subject I am reminded of that great statesman Horemheb way back in the XVIII Dynasty *[He was the last pharaoh of the 18th Dynasty of Egypt (1550–1295 BC)]*, who had the quality of being able to change his god, his master, his ideas, and his morality at a moment's notice. He was ambitious, farsighted, and able to see when he had made a mistake, and succeeded in making his own interests coincide with those of his country. In the course of his long life he showed the same versatility, and the same understanding of men, and happenings, through three reigns, and two revolutions, till he at last came to rule the country for 30 years, and in all circumstances he knew how to wait, with patience and good grace.

Saturday, May 14th, 1932.

Suffered the usual "pre-holiday-ante-work" feeling. Today is the hottest day we've had this year, after an early morning mist, the weather was of the kind commonly called heavenly. I gave way to Duncan, and we went birds nesting in Swaine woods, instead of my going to Otley Show. I had the satisfaction of climbing a decent tree and getting a magpie's nest in which there were seven eggs. Unfortunately I broke three of them in getting them down, and another in careless blowing. We also found half-a-dozen partridge eggs - and another of nature's tragedies - a stoat had discovered the nest. *[The practice of 'birdnesting' or 'nesting' and collecting wild birds' eggs was a common hobby, before being banned in the UK in 1954.]* Heard the Cuckoo for the first time this year.

Had Dinner at Duncan's. And spent the evening with Alice at Adel. Conversation very illiterate, and I bestowed my kisses more like deliberate insults.

Whit-Sunday, May 15th 1932.

I forgot to say yesterday that Duncan had bought some new gramophone records. They are all pretty good, but I single out "Goodnight Vienna" *[probably from the movie of the same name, it being released in March 1932]* as being the best.

In the afternoon, Lewis, Duncan and self again went nesting, this time to Leathley Woods. It was great fun and I enjoyed every minute of it. We must have found a score nests, but of the commoner types, chiefly, blackies, and thrushes with a couple of chaffinches, and wood pigeon.

Bill did not come with us. After the 'do' with Lewis last year on the Broads, they haven't spoken so much as half a dozen words to each other. I have avoided him for some weeks. His vast wealth has been getting overpowering. Maybe I have the inferiority complex. Maybe after a time he will turn out better, and a wiser man for his experience and money. I hope so - if only for the sake of past memories. When he chooses, he can reveal a very charming personality.

Came home, changed, dined at Duncan's off some very excellent ox-tail stew, and Stilton cheese, which was good, though I thought a trifle bitter. Having come to terms with one's stomach, and armed ourselves with a couple of cigars, and strolled up to the Hall Park, we listened to the band like civilised citizens.

Dear God, let me have a fine day tomorrow!

Whit-Monday, May 16th, 1932.

Today, has been the high-water mark. Everything has gone without a hitch, and has been excellent. Lewis, Gladys, Edith, Arthur, Duncan and self go off to Wensleydale. We had a picnic lunch, a few miles this side of Wensley - on the river bank. In the afternoon we walked to Bolton Castle, through the Park. The weather was ideal; mere words cannot express the charm of spring, and the charm of Wensleydale. Utopia, doesn't seem so very far away. I learn that Cooke-Yarborough's Dad, is Lord Bolton's agent. They have a delightful house on the estate.

Duncan found a Jackdaw's nest in which there were four young. We also found a waterhen's nest, in a

Hawthorn bush, at least five feet from the ground, which is surely rather remarkable.

Wild flowers were blooming in careless profusion: primroses, cowslips, anemonies, wall violets, wild violets and wild orchids.

We finished the day sensibly with a good old Yorkshire Ham and egg tea, at the Three Horse Shoes, Wensley. Oh, that flavour of the ham, and the unlimited supply of genuine moorland Wensleydale cheese! As Duncan aptly remarked: "Its all 'Honkey-Dorey'."

Lewis suggests that as I am about to spend about £25 / £30 on 'Minor' *[A popular British car known as a Morris Minor that came out in the late 1920's]*, I might get a decent model for that, plus the present 'Minor' in part exchange. But I say better a devil you know than one you don't.

Tuesday, May 17th, 1932.

In the morning we go Rook Shooting at Hawkesworth Hall; only 8 birds fell to my gun, but the birds were well on the wing. Mr. Guy Barrett says the correct time for rooks is between May the 13th, and May 16th, and this year they are pretty well forward owing to the warmth and the rain.

Lunched excellently at Fence End, then took Alice and Laura for a picnic tea in the woods above Norwood Edge. How those women bore me, and that's putting it mildly. If it wasn't for Duncan... but then that's the big difference between us. He has no principles in that direction.

Shouldn't be surprised if I catch cold as a result of the damp grass!

Wednesday, May 18th, 1932.

Tonight, I feel hellishly tired - probably the after effects of the holidays, and today I have been particularly dozy for I caught a 'Pudsey" *[a town near Leeds, West Yorkshire]* for a "Guiseley" tram *[another town in the borough of Leeds, West Yorkshire]*.

Thursday, May 19th, 1932.

Develop a slight sore throat. Went to Hull and saw Ralph Mead, who was pretty well down at the heels - what an appalling tragedy of good intentions. Gave him lunch and half a crown *[2 shillings and sixpence or about £10 today]*.

Friday, May 20th, 1932.

Events have always happened with a rush in my life. But tonight has brought an entirely new experience. Never before have I realised that a man could get into such a blue funk. Somewhere in my previous notes I believe I said that I'd never slept with a prostitute - Well, thank God that statement still holds. I was extremely weak to have given way to Duncan, and I deserve severe reproach on that score. The ribald crudeness amazed me. Duncan merely said to two doubtful looking young women on Commercial Street about 10.30 p.m. "...Hello beautiful." in that characteristic way of his, and before you could say Jack Robinson, the two of them were in the car, engaging in business-like conversation - involving me in a difficult mixture of inner fury and outer apology. I could hardly stand for I was mercifully very tight. Everything in the room was hazy, and it was damn badly lighted. All I could do was to keep a sickly grin on my face, and look foolish - though to appear foolish, at times, is the lot of the wise.

The great god Neuritis is doubtless saving up his thunderbolts.

Saturday, May 21st, 1932.

Today, I felt the reaction, I was physically sick all morning, and felt like nothing on earth, very disgusted and very disgruntled. It rained all day, putting an end to all our outdoor activities. Saw Lewis in the afternoon, recuperated, somewhat in the evening in the Smoke Room at Fence End with Alice and Laura - poodle faking *[he who makes a point of socialising with women; a ladies' man.]*, - and listening to the wireless. I am beginning to think that it would be a great mistake to overwhelm one by the attentions, which are a pleasure to so many.

Sunday, May 22nd, 1932. (Staying with Duncan).

Every minute of today has been golden. We set sail about nine forty-five a.m. in shorts, and complete with lunch and tea for a day's nesting in Nidderdale. In a spinney, just a little way past Blubber-houses, the gods favoured us with good fortune for we found a couple of deserted nests, and each had two eggs in, one was a chaffinch, and the other an ordinary hedge sparrow. The ground was still very wet after yesterday's heavy rain.

We lunched a belle etoile *[à la belle étoile - under the stars]* at Guisecliff Wood, near Patley Bridge; off some excellent Salmon Mayonnaise. We drew Guisecliff Woodland, but were lucky enough to see a couple of wild black rabbits - which are, I believe, pretty rare. And we had some good climbing practice, the giant rocks are very impressive. They rise up about eight hundred feet from the valley. And at the top a curious thing happens; by judicious distribution of ones body - one may, with the left-foot be in a desolate moorland, and, by turning your head to the right appear in a peaceful and fertile valley, with the little village of Patley at its head. From here we visited Bewley, and explored some of the streams at Dacre.

Saturday, May 28th, 1932.

What's to be done about it?

Today, I am turning my footsteps southwards to fair London Town, and lo! What do I find? It's all very difficult that I hardly know my own mind.

Betty loves me.

That's pretty staggering, isn't it? But I'm far too young to even think of marriage. I repeat myself, we see too little of each other to carry on a practical courtship, so Betty will try and get a job in Leeds. We mutely decided to marry somewhere in the distant future (that is to say nothing was actually said).

So I suppose I had better start and save... What a hope!

In the afternoon we went to Kew Gardens, many of the parts were very beautiful. But I am of the opinion, that we, speaking nationally, squander too much time and money on these public institutions. When a country is going through such a difficult time as ours, an effort should be made to curtail some of that expense.

In the evening we visit "Cavalcade", at The Theatre Royal, Drury Lane. It created a lasting memory. The funeral of Queen Victoria, the South African War, and The Tuesday, October 22nd 1918, are scenes which will never be forgotten. I almost think there is a spiritual side to it also; that the sight of the utmost limit of human endurance, and courage, is one which bears a lesson of its own.

To quote, our friend Mr. Virgil - "Bella! Horrida Bella!" - well, who wants war, with its bloody slaughter anyway? It's so futile!

After all, history was only written so that we may pass over the road to prosperity, once, and not many times.

Thursday, June 2nd, 1932.

Felt much better after having had a swim with Lewis.

What a magnificent type he is. His physical fitness excites my admiration; though the tinge of comparison is bitter. Afterwards, I pour out my woes regarding Betty's letter, which came yesterday morning and, as a climax is anticipated. This is what she said:-

"My dearest,

Tim, I have come to the conclusion, after a lot of thinking that the best thing for us would be to become engaged. I couldn't come up and get a job in Leeds unless we were engaged. It wouldn't be fair on Daddy, you see people would start saying: "How awful of Mr. Jackson to let his daughter come to Leeds", as it would be so very obvious why I had come. But if we were engaged it wouldn't be so bad, in fact, it would be the only natural thing for me to want to be near you. And, my dearest, I do want to be near you, and you know Tim, if you got fed up with me, it wouldn't be a very dreadful thing to break it off.

Oh! Tim how I hate to have to write all this to you, but it seems the only thing to do. We agreed we couldn't go on as we were - with an occasional visit to either Leeds or London, as the case may be.

If I could only tell you all this; it would be so much easier, but I can't, well, I must just make the best use of pen and paper.

Tim, if the money question seems to stop you, please don't let it. I don't care a row of pins about that, and I am just knowing that God always has been my supply, and yours, and he will always be. I should never be the least bit afraid of having enough and to spare. God has always given me enough - and he wouldn't stop quite suddenly. Also, if I came to Leeds you would have so much more opportunity of getting to know me so to speak.

I had a talk with Marie about it today. She was so very sweet and understanding, but she did show me that I couldn't come up to Leeds unless we were engaged. It wouldn't be fair to Daddy, to her, to myself, or to you for that matter. You see I don't want to be talked about too much. I am sure you would hate it for me.

Oh! Please do understand this, Tim, I just couldn't bear you not to understand, and hate me for it.

I so want a job in Leeds so very, very much, and I so want to be near you. But you do see don't you?

Oh! How I wish I had told you all this yesterday. But I'm afraid that I only had thought about it from my own point of view. I don't care a row of pins what people say, but it would be dreadful for Daddy, and for the rest of the family, especially as I haven't got a Mummie of my own, at least she isn't with me now.

Please will you write to me very very soon so that I shall be put out of my misery, because I do so hate having to write all this, but I do want to be fair to you, My dear, and its the only way. Tim, Please, Please, understand!

If you would like to come and talk about it. Do come down on Saturday - even if you cannot get a 'day trip', I'll fork out the necessary for you to come.

Oh! It's all so very difficult, and I do love you so very much, Tim. I don't know how fond you are of me; or if you feel that this would be altogether wrong. Please come and see me, or let me know. I should so hate you to let the money question keep us back, as I feel that to be so very wrong.

Anyway there would be no harm in our being engaged, and I, personally think long engagements are so very much better, as you can work together, and get to know each other, and so avoid those perfectly hateful mistakes.

Tim, do come and let us talk about it; if you would like to. I know its asking an awful lot of you to come down again so soon, but if you knew how unhappy I feel about it - I think you would come.

If only you knew how I want to help you. But I'm sure you must understand.

I'm sorry to have to bring things to a head so suddenly, but I simply cannot let things drift anymore and it isn't right for either of us.

Dearest Love, Yours as ever,

Betty.

Unless I'm very much mistaken that letter was written by a girl very much in love, and possibly by her emotion a little further than she might have wished. Nevertheless it is a charming letter.

Lewis tells me that I know my own business best - but he thinks that I should think twice before getting engaged. As he says, I don't even know the price of a load of coals yet.

Second thought...

My reply (after much brow wrinkling) eventually turned out as follows :-

My very dearest Betty,

I have spent two whole days, thinking as level-headedly as possible. But you know, my dearest, people only get engaged for one purpose - and I am sure that purpose is too far distant. I am equally sure that to make our engagement public would give more cause for Mrs Grundy

to wag her tongue. After all, I hardly know the price of a load of coals; if
you understand my meaning. And we are both so very young - rather in fact too young.

I, like you, want to be much nearer you. But I am sure if it is right some other way will be shown.

Before we took that step, I must have at least several hundreds tucked away - and a little more advanced towards my ambition, either at the head of Richard Nickols, or a super-sound position with Harold Nickols at Joppa, or setting sail for myself. You say that I have not to let the money question stand in our way. My dearest that would be impossible.

I, like you, wish we had had a bit longer chat than the few minutes we had in Kew Gardens. It is really all my fault. I'd meant to... but... somehow I was a bit shy; though that's rather a silly word to use. I was just too happy at being with you.

I have not told my Dad or Mother anything of this prospect; perhaps for the better or for the worse, but be that as it may. I should, of course have to talk it over with them first.

My dear, I do hope this will not increase your misery; it's making me feel pretty beastly too. I just have to re-read what I have written, and it seems pretty vague. It's the best I can do. I know you'll understand.

Love, as ever, thine,

Tim.

I hope I have made myself clear as to what was in my mind. I only give these letters in full - because in the future they may be more than just a passing interest.

Who knows?

Tuesday, June 21st, 1932.

Today, as I was travelling to Birmingham via Sheffield. I went through Chatsworth Park, and to my pleasant surprise the house was open to the Public so says I to myself: "This is too good a chance to miss".

I regret to record that our plutocratic Mansions leave me cold. The pictures, however, did impress me. The best were in the main Dining Hall. Another thing that irritated me was the way in which we were rushed through the bally place as though we were tourists, out for the day. This was a sharp contrast to the peaceful and beautiful gardens. We were given hardly any time to feast our eyes on any one thing for more than a few minutes. My whole body and mind revolts against conducted tours - being herded together like sheep.

Wednesday, June 29th, 1932.

At Wrekin.

Today, the weather has been the last word; an absolute ideal June day. I arrived in Wellington about 3.45 - just in nice time to get the inevitable awkwardness of recognition over before tea.

Today, being Wednesday was a half-holiday. And Wrekin is playing the Staffordshire Gentlemen - each side playing twelve men, and amongst the latter, Wilkie, the old Saxon. My word how that fellow has grown up, he is a picture of young British manhood. They have got the School all out for 155, and after tea they will bat.

A dainty tea is now being served beneath the welcome shade of the oak and sycamore trees behind the Grand Pavi - said he dropping back into the old slang! I had tea with Mr. Rolt (Fatty), and also met J. P. Ford, who has taken on the job as a temporary master. He is very aloof - hardly condescending to even acknowledge me. Tea is over, and Wrekin takes the field. Leisurely we find deck chairs, and settle down; greatly at peace with the world. Business worries seem to be as far away as the distant feathered clouds.

> The afternoon was warm, soft airs
>   were wafted by the breeze,
> When free from all 'leatherly' cares
>   I slumbered 'neath the trees.

The atmosphere was wonderful, not twenty yards away sits (and slumbers) our worthy founder - Sir John Bailey. I wonder what is passing through his mind as he surveys his handiwork? A dozen healthy young Britons, not yet hardened into the bone of manhood; being schooled in a system - which he has helped in no little way to strengthen.

Next to me sit Mr. & Mrs. Sawyer, (Fitzie), and Major B.C.W. Johnson, O.B.E., (Old Spit), who kept us well amused with his witty racontage on his visit to George, at Palace Buckingham, to get his distinction.

I was most impressed with the boys - what a topping lot they look, a lump came in my throat. God! If only some of those days could come over again! I hope they appreciate their luck, and enjoy their fleeting days to the full.

Middleton has just made a brilliant catch at slips. Should think he will get his 'colours' today. Wilkie is out for 11.

I like 'Fitz' Sawyers - as the best of the Masters. I like his dry humour. Mrs. Sawyers is a great sport, perhaps because she has had some children of her own. Incidentally, she had been only the day before to the Speech Day at Shrewsbury School, when His Royal Highness The Prince of Wales, had graced the School with His presence - in a none too new 'boater'. You know I always thought that the Hanoverians treated Mr. & Mrs. Sawyers pretty feebly; though I'm pleased they don't think so.

Ron showed me round the School - the same Chapel, but with the addition of two more stained glass windows. The same 'big school', the same 'gyms!' The same old 'cage', the same old "Newlands", though it goes under a much more dignified name now... "Bailey House". The same old swimming bath, in which there were about 30 boys splashing their young shrimp pink bodies about. I note that Windsor House, the New School, and the New Playing Fields, are very laudable additions.

I had the novel experience of hearing B.C.W.J. give a dictation class in his study at Norman House. What a deluge of memory came to mind.

And so to dinner. I am invited to dine with the masters - a very delightful experience. In the course of conversation about the Cricket Match, B.C.W.J. said, "...You know, whenever I see Wilkie; I cannot help thinking..."

"Whats that?" asked Ferdie.

"About the 'loose-boxes'" replied B.C.W.J.

And here the conversation ended, as suddenly as it had started. To me it was quite obvious that they were referring to the scandal of the 'loose-boxes' - that den of iniquity where that light sounding thing called 'romantic friendship' was practiced and prospered. Masters must, I suppose, recognise that sort of thing goes on in the dormitories, and realise that it is all part of a scheme.

After dinner I stroll round by the Cricket fields, alone with my thoughts and my pipe. What a glorious evening it is; cool, fresh, clear, yet warm. With the smell of newly mown grass, and the far off rattle of the mower. I feel very very happy.

The same chapel - the same service, it is very inspiring to hear 350 male voices, ably led by a well-tutored choir singing the hundred and fifth Psalm, for it is the twenty-second day of the month.

After this we say our farewells, and I enjoyed a glorious run to Stafford. With the shadows lengthening and the smell of hay-dew, and the gentle breeze I crossed the border into Staffordshire. "The peace of God - which passeth all understanding," descends!...

Thursday, June 30th, 1932.

This entry is written after my seventh crossing to Ireland. Never before in my life have I seen such a motley crowd of humanity. Kingsbridge Station, yesterday, and "Lady Munster", on the way home will always be unforgettable memories.

This religious mania that has swept Ireland is really remarkable. The Eucharistic Congress... Flags. Flags, everywhere; sprouting from tree tops, Mill Chimneys, and even tied to Railway signals.

From a business point of view, it has not been altogether satisfactory. I must develop more grit and character, and to myself I have a vague feeling that I was not a roaring success - by failing to draw an amicable agreement with the Lee people, and I hate indefinite things. I must stick out my jaw and stick like a limpet, when the hill is steep.

Still, I suppose it will turn out alright.

Monday, July 24th, 1932.

God, how wonderful!

I have paid Mr. Sykes of Wetherby a visit and ordered my riding breeches. I am letting you into a secret - because I have not breathed a word to anyone. The first thing they'll know (if you don't let on, that is) is to see me mounted in the [h]'untin' field. I fully appreciate what is said about 'little things'. But I cannot help that. It gave me a great thrill to discuss the finer points of tailoring, the cut of leggings, saddles, and boots, and of course, the cut of breeches. Sykes is definitely a good fellow.

Wonder in detached sort of way, what cousin Neil will have to say when he sees cousin Tim in exactly the same breeches - with the same exquisite cut. Bugger Rugger! This winter I mean to concentrate on riding and hunting. I mean to make a start during the coming Holidays at both Filey and Scarborough... 1 to find my seat ...then for the day-of-days.

"Your heart and your head keep boldly up,
Your hands and your heels keep down.
Your legs close to the horse's side -
And your elbows close to your own."

Friday, July 15th, 1932.

Another day has come and is about to fade into tomorrow. This day has been a decided red letter day. I have a terrific chance. The position is briefly:- At the end of the month, I cease to be employed by Richard Nickols. I am to go to Joppa. I suppose I have known this for twelve months, but for some reason I have always warned it off, and never really troubled about it. Consequently, it is a bit of a shock now.

Not until now have I realised how much I have to thank Mr. Clarkson, for the feeling that has existed; him for me, and me for him. Sounds almost sentimental, but the fact remains - I shall be very sorry indeed to leave Burley Mills.

Without any question of doubt, the 22 months I have spent at Burley, have been the happiest of my business career. What then; shall I think of them in years to come? I have developed in many directions - amongst the most important is a sense of thoroughness, and neatness and to no small extent a broader outlook on life.

Many of the men in the works have been topping to me this afternoon. They said they were very sorry to lose me. I suppose they realised that they owed their two months 'overtime', largely to my efforts. I am certain their farewells were genuinely meant. John Ross, and Fowler, the splitter, who both belong to that fast-dying type, the old fashioned British working fraternity, who blends thoughts, reserve, conscience, and a genuineness that is to be found nowhere else in the world. Burley Mills have several men belonging to this category. I shall not easily forget their parting wishes. Simple words, simply spoken.

One of my customers sent me a happy farewell this week, in the form of a 2,000 dozen order. My efforts have not been in vain. I also have the satisfaction of knowing that my job has been very capably filled by Stanley Barker of Otley. I spent this evening cleaning 'Minor'. I am just a little bit sad - but happy and at peace with the world.

Saturday, July 16th, 1932.

I want to try and write today's entry in simple English - with no cheap comparatives and superlatives. Well here goes:

(a) Joppa - the great interview has come and gone, and I was in a blue funk. However, the sum and substance of it is that I am to understudy Mr. Bruce. Apologies for entering into personalities, but I am not subordinate to, but to work in conjunction with Mr. Blockey and Mr. Bottomley. Mr. Bruce paid me many compliments, whilst Major Harold said that I had only myself to thank for the opportunity that was being offered. Mr. Bruce, returning to the subject, said they wanted a man who was not afraid of work, and whose thought was not everlastingly for himself.

My financial remuneration continues unchanged at £250, until they see how I settle. It will be like going back to school again. The end of the month will see me in my fifth position.

(B), and B stands for Betty. This afternoon I took Gweneth and her boating at Wetherby, which was extremely unsatisfactory. We had, however, a few minutes at the end of the day. It is quite clear that she wants some understanding from me, and I don't altogether blame her. Do I, or do I not want her in Leeds? Honestly, I don't know. Perhaps I am undeveloped, but I've never felt, for instance, the way Lewis feels towards 'em. Most certainly I intend to get married, but not before I am thirty. And that's a long time to ask any girl to wait for a fellow. She says she'll even go to Lands End for me. She's crazy. I'm in a fix. Blast it; to hell with love.

(c), is the happiest of the lot. My riding breeches have come. They are absolutely wonderful, and so they ought to be for £3. 10. 0. *[about £275 today]*. This week I have ordered myself a pair of boots, from one of the best firms in Northampton town. When in Leicester this week I purloined one of Dad's books W.J. Miles' "Practical Farriery" *[Published 1892, a complete guide to all that relates to the horse; its history, varieties, and uses, breaking, training, feeding, stabling, and grooming, how to buy, keep and treat a horse in health and disease]*, and also Mr. Scarth Dixon's, "The History of The Bramham Moor Hunt" *[1898]* - an edition that was limited to two hundred copies.

August, 1932, Camping at Filey.

I am starting these notes on the second day of Camp. I am just getting up, and still in my pygamjims, and it's a quarter to twelve. The excuse for this unseemly behaviour is that at 6.15 it started to rain. And I thought 'A Very Big Thought' (to quote Pooh Bear). I was snugger, and certainly drier in my flea bag, listening to the rain dripping on (and through) the tent, and the cries of the gulls.

Then I roused myself with the tune "What makes you so adorable?" Outside, everything looks very uninviting, the grass is heavy and sodden with rain. Thank heavens, my clothes, gramophone, and blankets are more or less dry, or only slightly damp.

TWO DAYS LATER.

Cheers and louder cheers! The weather seems to be taking up. I am sitting on the edge of the cliff. Through the field glasses I can see distinctly three anglers on the Brigg - coming round the Bay; I can just see the golden-salmon of St Oswald's glittering as the sun catches it. The beach looks very crowded. Can see the top of the gasometer *[huge cylindrical gas containers where gas was stored prior to distribution to the customer. We now use high pressure pipes to send directly.]*, so can place the station quite easily. A chap has just driven up the fairway of the fifteenth, but cannot see his ball. Some of the bungalows at Primrose Valley, and in 'the wilderness' - (of old) - look very spick and span. But, oh! What a blot on the landscape. Turning southwards: Ye Gods what a view! The sun is just catching the white chalk cliffs of Speighton and Bempton. How impressive they look. Several people keep disappearing and reappearing as they dodge between the big rocks, in their attempt to reach the old submarine, which from here looks just like a big black beetle lying in its back - helpless.

I cannot describe the sea decently, owing to the low haze. There is a small cargo boat - but too far out to see well. There are several fishing smacks snuggling beneath Father Briggs parental care.

Last evening I had supper out in the moonlight - sitting round my fire with a plate of excellent stew upon my knees.

Camp, on the whole has been rather disappointing, as I've had only one fine day out of eight.

FOUR DAYS LATER.

I have had a couple of rides. To be astride a horse again after all these years gave me an unutterable thrill. One of my pet ambitions seem a little nearer fulfilment. The first ride was only on the sands at Filey. The second was worth every penny of the ten bob it cost. It was one of Tom Shaws horses of Scarborough. Ernest Roper, his groom laddie took us by Throxenby Hall, Raincliffe Woods, and so, on to the top of Forge Valley, returning via the old Toll road. It was great, and the weather ideal. Roper let us have a bit of jumping over fallen trees etc: and we had one good gallop.

Wednesday, August 10th, 1932.

My reception at Joppa has been rather similar to what you would have expected from a cold storage warehouse. I have been there two 'never-ending' days. Bottomley hasn't even condescended to say "Good morning" yet, but Mr. Blockey genuinely said "Welcome to Joppa" on Monday morning. Whilst in the warehouse, never by any chance does Tommy Bailey, the head warehouseman, tell me anything. I have to ask all questions, and then, only get crusty replies, which makes my position none the easier.

I must stick to it however, and carry out my duties with a deep sincerity, and enthusiasm, and make an honest effort to radiate Love, Life, and Truth, and inso doing I feel that my efforts will not go by unheeded.

Let me put those glorious days of Burley behind - for they have gone forever.

Friday, August 26th, 1932.

This evening I had a chat with Mr. Bruce re: Evening Classes, and I suggested the following:-

Languages (French or German),

Boot and Shoe Manufacture,

Leather Industries (The University)

Book Keeping and Shorthand, or,

Junior Accountancy.

Mr. Bruce thought that either French or Shorthand would be the most useful.

But he added that a great deal depended upon me! That I could teach myself much - by my own efforts, more; in his opinion, than by going in for actual class instruction. For instance: read, mark, learn and inwardly digest all the Trade Papers, and concentrate with what was in hand - meaning, of course, that I should master my environment, and Joppa's system (if any).

He added that it was the wish of both Mr. Noel and Mr. Harold that I should be in possession of all facts, and an all-round working knowledge of 'us' Tan yard processes.

After this, he said, possibly as an afterthought - something that has set me by the ears, when he was delivering his bitter judgement against theoretical chemistry in a Tan Yard. It was this, ad verbatim: "...if you were given a pack of greenhides, could you produce a passable full chrome leather?... If you want to study something. Keep your knowledge fresh on the subject. I have something at the back of my mind. These are not idle words. Now off you go, and think over what I have said..."

I wonder what he really did mean.

Saturday, August 27th, 1932.

Today, we have had our first Rugger Practice of the season - 'midst glorious and brilliant sunshine. The whole thing was rather absurd. The lack of enthusiasm was very evident. There was no one to direct our energies. Duncan and Cunnington each scored a handful of tries amidst complete apathy.

Still it's grand to be amongst the chaps again.

Sunday, August 28th, 1932.

"What of this life if, so full of care,
We have no time to stand and stare ?
No time to stand beneath the boughs
And stare as long as sheep and cows?
No time to see, when woods we pass
Where squirrels hide their nuts in grass ?
No time to see, in broad daylight,
Streams full of stars, like skies at night?
A poor life is this, so full of care
We have no time to stand and stare" -

W . H .　　D a v i e s .

[Collected Poems of W H Davies, 1916]

Saturday, September 17th, 1932.

Has been a wonderful day, more like April than September. Played rugger against Cleckheaton, on their soil. Mr. Hugh Curry, the ex-county cap 'refferd'. He was great. I played quite a decent game, though I say it as shouldn't. Anyway, it made me feel very cheery afterwards, and it put quite a rosy complexion on life.

Yesterday, I paid another visit to Mr. Sykes of Wetherby to get measured for my leggings. We argued for nearly an hour and a half, as to whether they should be of leather or Box Cloth, and the pros and cons of a riding boot. A b a d boot can look just as silly as a human being, and, generally one of their worst faults is a lack of length in the leg.

Sunday, October 1st, 1932.

Rained like hell in the morning, but it took up in the afternoon, and was glorious. Went with Duncan for a grand walk to Otley, via West End, Long Stoop, then cut across country to Surprise View, and so down to Otley. Duncan is great company, and has an equal sense of humour. This afternoon he spilt a very cheery suggestion, that we start a 'once-a-week' men's Bridge four.

Life is full of disappointments, whilst at the time they loom pretty large, they may, (and I hope), turn out to be only mole hills in the long run. I had fully expected being up at The Leather Fair for the whole week, so when Bruce informed me on Friday that I was only to go for three days, I thought it was rotten. What it is to come down a peg. Still I may as well make the best of it, and the most of a slender opportunity.

The last four weeks at Joppa has gone very slowly, so possibly, here is a chance of justifying the 'Nickols-Bruce' confidence in me.

Another of life's knotty little problems is Betty. This week I have had a letter from Mrs. Jackson, actually deciding for me, (if you please!), that I should make "The White House", at Barnes, my headquarters whilst in town. I have quite decided to have it out with her... that we both must be considered free, though I realise with a bitter regret that when you exchange a romance for a friendship; you exchange the sky for a ceiling, but it cannot be helped.

I shall not make another entry before next Sunday Evening… and I wonder what sort of a tale I shall have to tell then.

Sunday, October 9th, 1932.

What a pleasant change this week has provided. It has done me all the good in the world to be amongst some of the leather chaps again. You know there is a certain charm about the Leather Trade, it sort of gets you.

It has been only a moderately successful week, it has made me realise one thing - that my position at Joppa is going to take a very long time to consolidate - if ever.

At the moment my mind is full of improvements that I would effect at Joppa when I get the reins of government, but when will that come about? As it is I am never given a job of any description. True enough I am entirely my own master - wandering round as I please, picking up what I can. But being made to feel such small beer and so very insignificant goes very much against my grain. At the fair itself, Mr. Bruce introduced me to perhaps half a dozen customers, otherwise I went by unnoticed.

I must pull myself together, and not let this inferiority complex get the better of me. I must make a more determined effort to convert my leisure into a more useful training for the future, for who knows what it holds? I refer to French, Shorthand, mastering English précis and style, and generally buck myself up!

At last it has come. Betty gave me a lovely lead by pressing me for a weekend at Barnes, to which I answered that my acceptance would only indicate an engagement, or in other words 'an affaire complet', and, of course, that is entirely out of the question. Atmosphere becomes positively tense. Betty wants to stop writing and have her photograph back and all sorts of things. Eventually we come to reason... to continue, but on condition we tell each other the moment there is anyone else.

And as there's nothing more to say, I'll close.

October 22nd, 1932.

Tonight, the eve of my 24th Birthday, and I am feeling almost on the verge of despair. Will I ever have anything to do at Joppa? I am sick and tired of being at a loose end, and being so insignificant. I am beginning to think 'the fair' was a complete wash out.

I wonder, if, after all I was a bloody little fool ever to have left Burley, where at least I had authority at my finger tips, and the environment was both cheery and happy, and we all worked as a team. But of course there was absolutely no means of foreseeing what is not taking place. It is most unfortunate. But there we are - the milk is spilt, or I've made my own bed, which ever you like.

Tonight, I feel that it would have been better to have remained a big fish in a little pond; than be a little fish in a big pond as I am at present.

October 29th 1932.

Concentration is the secret of success, together with an infinite capacity for taking pains.

Must master absolutely EVERY detail of our own production and also the why's and wherefore's.

There is no doubt at all, that if I want to get on, I must be more brisk in my decisions: and not forget that familiarity breeds contempt. It is never wise to be too rational - it always argues. Democracy may either be a great system under strong leadership, or, a suicidal system under feeble leadership.

November 7th, 1932.

I have just come to the end of an extraordinary week. It has all been such a rush, that all my thoughts are still muddled. Let me jot them down, then sort out the jumble afterwards:

Port, Beagling, Bursting Balloons, Beechams. j'em ai un, scudding, scratting, and unhairing with George, and so it goes on.   The announcement in yesterday's "Yorkshire Post":-

Golden wedding.
CHEETHAM - COUPLAND., November 7th 1882 at Henshaw Church, by The Rev. Nasseau Clarke, Joseph,

the fourth son of Christopher Cheetham of Horsforth to Lena, youngest daughter of William Coupland, Bolton House, Yeadon.

Mother, Dad, and Barbara come up from Leicester, for our little party of celebration. Dear old Ogre made his little speech and burst 'his balloon', we all had our turns, and it was great fun.

The next paragraph, if correctly labelled would read "Unhairing by hand in '32" Peter Nickols is coming to Joppa for about 6 weeks - to go through the Tannery to get the run of things. So says I to myself, here is an opportunity, for a few weeks at any rate, to break the monotony of the warehouse, and it's not to be missed. I get my director's permission, and I sojourn down the 'Yard' at Joppa. What a fine type of man the tanning trade attracts. George, my mate, is a particularly likeable chap, tough as a lion, yet quiet and simple in his tastes, and genuine to the tips of his fingers. Roughing it, as I am having to do, is making me feel quite lusty, and I learn a thing or two about human nature, and the working man's psychology.

At first, Unhairing, is far more awkward, than actually difficult. There is a considerable art in keeping the hide central to the beam, and being able to 'work' it easily on the backward stroke. Another point is to have a good bolster, and an easy backing. Incidentally, I learn that a tremendous amount of time and money is spent very uneconomically in trying to acquire that skill which is the aim of practice.

This week also, I have been up to Oakfield Terrace, and entertained liberally. I have started my French classes (private tuition), I like Madame Dienar, she has quite a pleasant sense of humour.

But where on earth do the Beechams come in?

Lets move on to Armistice Day, November 11th. It brought a flood of memories back to me, as it did, no doubt to countless thousands. This two minutes Silence is getting a bit meaningless - a horribly sacrilegious thing to say. But what does it convey to me? The War stands for very little in my life. This years commemoration has been spent very oddly... leaning against a bateing paddle, surrounded by my respectfully silent workmates, and dripping hides. Only the trickling of water broke the silence. Curiously enough I couldn't bring myself to pray. I found myself wondering what was fat Amos's capacity for beer, and Amos was one of my workmates of colossal girth. And having solved that little problem, I found my mind running backwards. A year ago today (1931), I was at this precise moment being gloriously sick on the middle platform of Dundalk Station on my Third Irish Visit.

Two years ago today. I was having my finger bandaged in the top warehouse at Burley Mills. I was being initiated into the mystical and magical process of rounding kips. At two minutes to eleven I cut myself. I still have a scar on my left thumb.

Three years ago today (1929), I was in the dear old Ford, travelling to Wakefield for Mr. Gate. I stopped not, neither did I pray.

Four years ago today (1928), I was at Steads. I remember feeling very nervous of what to do, so I went to the lavatory for a smoke.

Five years ago today (1927), I spent in City Square, Leeds. At the time I felt rather awe-struck.

Six years ago today (1926), I had just left Wrekin. I was my own boss, at Newlay, and as I could think of nothing else better to do, I wandered into the Chemy Laboratory for a cigarette (Oh, those far off days).

Seven years ago today (1925), was undoubtedly spent in the Chapel at Wrekin College.

Before that I cannot remember.

On November 12, another ambition is realised, I go Beagling with the Airedale Pack. It was great. I mean to go again. Today's meet was at Leathley Church. The hounds moved off behind Leathley Hall. Robin, the Whip, is a great fellow, and has a very bonny way with the hounds.
Unfortunately, there were too many hares about, as their scents were getting continually crossed. I spent most of my time with Harry Jowett.

It is a thrilling sight to see 16 pairs of hounds in full cry. There was a continuous drizzle and it was very mild. We did not kill and we returned to Leathley about four o'clock.

The Luxury of a good hot bath, after hard exercise always provokes melody in man. A good dinner, good Port, a good Cigar, a few good tunes on the gramophone. (One in particular was very haunting "Love is the Sweetest Thing") a good book, and my easy chair in the smoke room at Woodbottom, is in my opinion just about as near to an earthly Utopia as is possible.

Saturday, December 3rd, 1932.

My dear Cyril,

I have purposely delayed answering your last letter (dated November 13th) until after my visit to Wrekin.

Last Saturday, I journeyed thither, and arrived in Wellington in time for lunch at The Charlton. As I drove up Constitution Hill I suffered the same oppression of spirit that I did in the old days when returning from the holidays. Now, as I believe you know I rather fancy myself at Rugger, so, verily I wrote to Split Johnson and asked for a game - nearly six weeks ago, and he graciously replied that he would be charmed if I could turn out;so when I arrived up at The School about two o'clock and found that there was no game for me... To say that I was peeved puts it very mildly. So I had to content myself with watching a very scrappy game, cursing, and nearly getting frozen stiff into the bargain.

After this, we had a belated tea in the Senior dining hall, but nevertheless   welcome, as it helped me to thaw. The General meeting was then held in the Saxon House room, (The old Chemy lab., as we knew it). A resolution was passed that the old Wrekinian Association should present the school with two squash courts, costing a maximum of £1200. *[Visiting there recently, I note that it was built, but since demolished around 2020.]*

I then returned to The Charlton, and dressed for dinner. Having a couple of Sherries, I once more set forth up Constitution Hill. The dinner was definitely good, and, being young I split a bottle of 'phiz', to help me through the speeches. Maxie as usual with characteristic vitality.

Reggie Howatt (Tudor), (I expect you will remember him, he was a pal of L.A. Thorpe's) spoke exceedingly well.

Fatty Rolt, asserting that he felt rather like a 'Yo-yo', wittily replied to one of the toasts. All the same I think the Old Boys do's are a lot of eye wash. Out of nearly 700 members, only 120 turned up, which, I think, is pretty lousy.

The meeting broke up, and many reassembled until the small hours in the warmer atmosphere of The House Masters Studies. I went to Higgs Walker, of Windsor House, and not to Hanover as you might have expected. Here, Horlicks flowed freely, and beer was offered to the more venturesome. About 1.30, I wandered back to the Charlton, where a very hearty party was in progress. Do you remember Glossop Thorpe? He was there and on the height of his form. Eventually I turned in about three.

Sunday morning I went to Chapel. The service was excellent. Not that I wish to appear a religious sort of a cove, but I appreciated it more than anything else. It seemed the most permanent.

After which I went back to The Charlton for luncheon, and retraced my steps again to dear old Yorkshire.

I hear a lovely bit of scandal about Bobbie Byass... that he got chucked out of Repton, and had divorced his charming young wife, and now earns a precarious sort of living playing at 'Journalism'.

By the way, you are a silly old ass if you go and get married. I know, only too well, that it's not easy to say "No", but you must dig up the necessary courage from somewhere.

That's the lot,

Ever, thine,

December 10th, 1932.

Much water has passed beneath the bridges since my last entry. The chief concern being Joppa. Today, I've had as long a chat with Mr. Harold as ever I've had since I've been there.   When I peg out I think I'll have a single word epitaph "...Inconsistency". Up to now everything connected with me has been odd, and God; Joppa's full of it. I am told that Mr. Blockey is shortly leaving us... which will leave the position of Works Manager vacant. Mr. Harold even went so far as to say he would back me up if I could do it, run the place myself. But for the time being I think it best to lie low and bide my time. I can pleasantly spend my time ferreting out the numerous irregularities - noting them, and learning all I can about production costs, and generally try to equip myself to take the utmost advantage of any opportunity when it rolls along.

With the office as damply friendly, as Bottomley, and the Warehouse as drily hostile - there is a rough passage ahead, but to progress is to conquer the seemingly impossible.

Another snag will be the dealing with the Noel-Harold complex?

Where should I begin? - In my own mind I think the Ware-house is the worst managed department in the whole tannery. To start some sort of order-routine book will be a great joy, and to give the Bailey Family the hard word, and telling them all to get a move on will be another. They're so damnably lazy!

The shedding question is another that needs close attention. Getting the bridges covered is one of my suggested improvements. In fact, Bruce is perfectly right for once when he says... greater attention must be paid to detail throughout the tannery.

The whole place needs cleaning to make brighter and more spontaneous working conditions.

Then there is the problem of = "'baccy time" *[smoking break]*, which is admittedly rather essential. The economising of electric power, and a better working combination between the 'yard' and the Warehouse, are other notes on my list. Often, I like to try and analyse the number of distinct movements in a process, and, if you study them for a few moments you can nearly always find some way of reducing the existing number. Economise the skill (and money) of skilled labour by replacing the labouring part of the job with a labourer.

And whilst warmed up to it, lets consider the general spirit of the worker as it is both a vital and vast problem. There is something ironical about the man that will spend all his energy on a Saturday afternoon playing football... that his side may win, and he will struggle on to that end even though bleeding and bruised, and covered with mud - and almost to his last gasp, and yet on Monday morning, show a very different spirit, and, may in fact prove himself to be a slacker and a shirker. It is universally admitted that there is a tendency for play - one cannot help wondering what has happened to such tendency for work, which there undoubtedly was a generation ago. I think that the football spirit is worth cultivating in the factory.

Christmas 1932.

I can hardly let this weekend slip by without some sort of record, because within a few hours it has become very memorable. What a Christmas it has been! I started in good style at The Heaton Tennis Club Dance with Margaret Gate, and it was a good show - definitely, the time "Lets put out the lights..." is still running through my brain. Saturday saw me travelling southwards, arriving in Leicester in time for tea. Felt very tired, so I went to bed early. Christmas day; opened with the usual ceremony of opening presents from eight o'clock onwards. Mum and Dad gave me a topping shooting stick - just what I was wanting, and apart from ten bob from Auntie Gertie, that is all I got. Still I'm not grumbling because I've had my fling. I only hope that Barbara does as well as I have done.

The events of Monday and Tuesday made all the foregoing festivities look very pale.

I meet one Tim Muxworthy, who has come to stay with the Boulters. I was magnetised. He's a great laddie, his principles of life revolve round hunting, cubbing *[training young hounds to kill foxes by targeting their cubs]*, beer, and plenty of it, rugger, and reading Surtees, and more beer to finish with.

On Monday; Tim, Leigh and self decided to follow the Quorn, sheltered from the elements by the luxury of The Boulters very old Clyno *[The Clyno car was a nine years' wonder on the British market. The Clyno marque rose to pre-eminence in the market in 1926, becoming the third most popular manufacturer, and as swiftly declined].* Eventually we ended up at Six Hills for an odd jar... before very long, Tim had surrounded us with grooms, second horseman and chauffeurs to the plutocratic members of The Quorn Hunt. Tim scored a terrific success with "The Old Sow". It was really a wonderful show - ending up by us all getting bidden to The Grooms Hot Pot Supper - such is the power of one man's enthusiasm. We got back to Leicester somehow, though I don't quite know how - tight as lords.

To let them go back to the Boulters in that state would have spelt disaster, so I had no alternative but to take them to "Braybrooke". Dad was splendid, he looked after us just as a Father should, filling us with food, black coffee, with a tact that is peculiar to men. After a bath, we were more or less alright again by eight o'clock feeling rather like death served up warm.

The Boulters party was absolute perjury.

Tuesday morning touched the peak. The three of us went to Narborough... to Mr. Brown's "....the bloke 'wot owns them 'osses". It was hyper super. I had a topping mount, a bay horse, just under 15 hands, game as anything, but she took some holding. The partnership between man and horse, teaches man a lot about the basic things of life - which under modern condition we might easily ignore.

Nothing, I swear in this world feels finer than that exhilaration that comes of a good gallop, especially after a couple of 'Rums' at Mr Brown's expense.

130

I have a mind to write Brown and send him a few shillings with the instructions to wire me if there is a Saturday meet anywhere near Narborough, with the South Atherstone. Then for the promised Day of Days.

In the afternoon I went with the old man to watch The Barbarians play Leicester, and saw some good open rugger. Leicester were beaten 22 - 10.

I'm afraid all our eyes were a little moist when it came to saying good-bye. I was very loathe to start, and had a funny lump in my throat. And with all sincerity I say, "...God bless them all."

January 4th, 1933.

I have come to a definite decision, I am not going to run 'Minor', my little car this quarter, I simply cannot afford it.

Thursday, February 9th, 1933

When going to work this morning, I both heard and saw the skylark in full song. It is remarkable what optimism, cheeriness, and hope can spring from such small things.

Monday, March 22nd, 1933.

Yesterday, was the first day of spring, and today looks as though it were really true. It is a glorious day. A fine spring day, is surely nature's best tonic.

I am moved to do two things, one abnormal, and the other quite normal.

The abnormal thing is that I go to Kirkstall Abbey during my luncheon hour. I wander up the naive in solitude, and out into the cloisters, which look quite inviting in the brilliant spring sun. I have done this to get the setting, conducive to a peaceful mind, so I can commit these thoughts to paper.

I have the Abbey to myself. I can see nothing romantic or startling… a couple of wastepaper baskets, and a notice "Please keep off the grass". Everything-else is in harmony for the time of the year. The grass looks a little greener, and the jackdaws are making a raucous row with their mating, and now and again I can hear the odd pigeon cooing. Really the only abnormal thing about this excursion is that I might have done it anytime during the last ten years… and yet because its on my own doorstep, so to speak, I've never done it.

The three months that have been drawing to a close have been particularly unexciting.

To give my tale continuity. Joppa continues highly unsatisfactory. To while away the time, I have started a sports club, with Mr. Harold's warm approval, and with Mr. Bruce's luke-warm support. So far it has availed nothing, but may have far reaching effects later.

The other day I asked Mr. Bruce, when I was to start travelling. He answered with his customary evasiveness that I should be getting my chance in the not far distant future. Oh, how typical!

My affair with Betty is gradually receding into the past. Our letters are taking on a strictly conventional form. Anyway, I've learnt my lesson.

Turning to Finance, things are going from bad to worse. I have sold my bit of War Loan for my insurance *[A 5% War Loan 1929 to 1947 issued in 1917 as part of the unprecedented effort by the government to raise money to pay for the First World War]*. Have given up all hope of saving. In another ten days I shall have my little car on the road again.

Everything at Woodbottom continues unchanged. Once Grannie gets an idea into her head, and some of them are funny ideas, no power on earth will shift them. Yes verily, it is easier to get water out of a stone than to get Grannie to change her mind. Again I am brought to realise that no true happiness ever comes from insisting on one's own way.

Have got a trifle fed up with rugger just lately. Either I get an official position with the club or I am packing it up. Lewis' rugger is going from strength to strength, and has been 'capped' three times this year.

Bill Irwin arrives back from his South African journey on April Fools Day.

My French classes continue, and are outrageously expensive, and I think on the whole are worth it. I must finish the job off properly, and go to France for my holidays this year.

Auntie Gertie has had a seizure, this week and is not expected to recover.

A new Society has been formed in Leeds, called The Leeds Round Table, I have joined. The object being to develop self-confidence for public speaking, and to study the science of citizenship, and so we go on... merrily because it is the second day of spring, and I am sitting in the sun, in the cloisters of Kirkstall Abbey.

April 17th, 1933. EASTER.

To those who know me, it does not matter what I look like. And to those that don't; it does not matter either.

I am staying with Mrs. Mead at Scarborough.

I am sitting on the style - at the top of Jacob's Ladder... *[Jacob's Ladder is a bridleway between Kinder Scout plateau and the hamlet of Upper Booth in the Vale of Edale, in the Derbyshire Peak District of England. In the 18th century Jacob Marshall farmed the land at Edale Head, at the top of what became known as Jacob's Ladder]* happy as the day is long. Sitting here, I am partly sheltered from a coldish wind - but basking in the brilliant March sun - even though it is the middle of April. At my side is Chris (Chris is a Bedlington *[Terrier, dog]*), who is licking my hand as I write these few notes.

It has been a jolly Easter, it makes me very happy to be running 'Minor' again.

Mrs. Mead has given me a couple of quid for riding, and all told I have had seven hours with quite a bit of jumping. I think I am improving.

A year ago today brings back memories - What Ho!

Wednesday, April1 19th, 1933.

Uncle Walter dies.

Thursday, April 20th, 1933.

Rooks, or are they Magpies (or crows) are building in the trees at the back of Woodbottom.

Friday, April 21st, 1933.

Uncle Walter is taken, with a great deal of fuss, to lie in state in Guiseley Church. Such is the price of fame.

Saturday, April 22nd, 1933.

Today's funeral is the only one where I have felt really sentimental.

View day at St. Helens Leather Works (Sale on Tuesday). My word the place looks a wreck.

Pay a flying visit to a Cricket Practice at Burley Mills.

Duncan gets very tight - Bill and I put him to bed.

Altogether, it has been quite a crowded day!

Sunday, April 23rd, 1933.

An excursion to Leicester. I couldn't help thinking as we passed through Sheffield that the view one gets from the train - is one of England's saddest sights. On the way home I read Whyte-Mellville's "Market Harborough" *[1890]*.

I paid a nocturnal visit to Newlay - bringing an old spade from the Stables. An interesting and incidentally quite a useful memento.

Tuesday, April 24th, 1933.

The final curtain at Newlay, and it was a good thing that Father was not there to see it descend.

The Bohemians Annual General Meeting at The Vesper. Duncan is elected Captain of the first fifteen, and I am elected skipper of the "A" XV. Actually the meeting was a bit of a fiasco. My carefully prepared speechlet was not required. To have the responsibility of leadership at one's elbow is good. It is one of my fétiche *[charm, (noun) something believed to have the power of magic or good luck]*.

Wednesday, April 25th, 1933.

The Leeds Leather Fair. I met a Mr. Chapman from Leicester - quite a smart fellow, and when introduced, he said he'd heard quite a lot about me, some good and some not so good. I burned with curiosity. In fact I am toying with the idea of becoming an abstainer.

Apparently more people know Tom Fool than Tom Fool knows.

Thursday, April 26th, 1933.

The swallows arrive at Woodbottom.

Friday, May 5th, 1933.

Heard the cuckoo for the first time this year.

The swallows are definitely building in the barn where I keep the car, and they are building directly above it. They are doing their stuff alright.

Saturday, May 6th, 1933.

I am involved in the vortex of war - the battlefield is arranged thus:-

The Split Warehouse has been the most unsatisfactory department in all the dissatisfaction of Joppa ever since I've been there, and lately it has been getting even more out of hand; so much so that a few days ago Teddy Bailey and his two lads spent ten hours (including two hours of overtime) to tie up ten bales. When Bottomley is away travelling Mr. Bruce is always more amiable towards me so I told him my tale of woe, and when he learnt that Teddy was some 12,000 splits behind hand with his work, Mr.

Bruce took a dive in at the deep end. An alteration is obvious. All this happened yesterday afternoon.

[In the tannery, a hide is 'split' in large machines while it is still wet. A skin is divided into several layers over the entire surface in a process called "splitting".]

So, this morning I caught Mr. Bruce before he went into the office, and asked him if I could have the responsibility of that warehouse, and he replied that something on those lines had been running through his mind - spoken in his best evasive manner, for which he is a past master.

Later in the morning he tells me that I am to have the responsibility at any rate until June 30th, when some sort of ground will be mapped out for me.

Monday, April 8th 1933.

Today, has been a very bitter pill. Mr. Bruce neither confirmed Saturday's conversation with either Bottomley or the Bailey family - though of course they must have known all about it. Today they exasperated me. I have been played off, firstly against one, then against the other. For instance Bottomley has been in the warehouse with various instructions - four times - and each time to young Bailey, and taking no bloody notice of me, and in return Bailey has been going over my head with numerous petty fogging queries to both Bottomley and Bruce, whom I feel has rather let me down.

As I see it there are six alternatives open to me:-

(1) Ask Mr. Bruce to confirm it all round.

(2) Tell Bottomley, and the Bailey that I am O.C. and that I will have no hole and corner work.

(3) Put some ginger at Bailey's behind, and just go ahead on my own.

(4) Wait with patience and as much grace as I can muster for things to straighten themselves in the washing.

(5) Tell the whole bloody lot to go to bloody hell. (That's how I feel at the moment, but I fear not very tactful.)

(6)Take the line of least resistance, and let things wander where they will, and this is what will probably happen.

Tuesday, May 9th, 1933.

Have another bit of a dust with Tommy Bailey, re the checking of some Shoulder Flesh Bales, when he and Billy (who is a little odd) practically accused me of rubbing some weights off the board.

I know it's so easy to be wise after the event, I ought to have raised hell, and told them it was a very serious thing to accuse a man of such deceitfulness, and stuck out for an apology.

Afterwards I have a tiff with Bottomley, who told me I was always interfering, and treading on his toes, and that one day I should be getting my fingers bunt. What an appalling tragedy of good intentions.

Oh, bloody hell.

Thursday, May 18th, 1933.

I have a slight accident with 'Minor' at West Park, Headingley - nobody was hurt - all the same it is a bloody nuisance. Did not lose my head for a second. But I have come to the conclusion to sell 'Minor' for several business-like reasons thus:-

(1) It costs at least 30/- a week to run her, and at the moment I am not getting 30/- worth out of her.

(2) I have three damned good friends with nine cars between them, and with their kindness I have little need for 'Minor', for social purposes and there does not seem much chance of my running her for the firm - as at Burley Mills.

(3) I fancy that the directors of Harold Nickols Limited, do not altogether approve of their staff supporting motors, and/or the possibility of my getting a rise is somewhat remote, I shall have to pull in, so there it is.

(4) Tax, £4; and Insurance, £9; both fall due at the end of the month, and I don't feel like renewing these on the eve of my holidays.

Finally, I don't feel justified in running a car.

Saturday, May 27th, 1933.

It has been said, I forget by whom, that the process of shaving provokes thought, and this morning I got rather a nasty jolt. There is, unfortunately, no doubt about it. My face was white and pinched, and my mouth dropped towards the corners.

The strain of the last two months have been telling on me. There is no doubt that I have created a bit of a stir with my reorganisation of the warehouse, and in the process I have made myself thoroughly unpopular - because I have found out what a lazy lot of slackers they are, and I am endeavouring to make them do a bit of work.

But what has hurt my feelings the most is the way Bruce has snubbed me - several times he has been into the warehouse this week and just ignored me - that's the worst of being so sensitive.

I have been working my guts out to get the place into some semblance of order for stocktaking at the end of June. I have been going down at seven in the morning, and sometimes stopping as late as seven in the evening and there's never even been a word of recognition.

Well, I ask you what is the use of caring? It's an almost unbelievable story of miscalculation.

One of the first signs of deterioration is I suppose neglect of one's appearance - you know, not being so particular about the shine of one's shoes, and I have been guilty of making a collar do for two days, and going to Joppa in flannel bags.

The high ideals I held about working as a team, and 'esprit de corps' are slipping away.

The possibility of my receiving any promotion of salary this year seems very unlikely. These last few weeks I have been so utterly miserable that once or twice I have caught myself up with a jerk for my thoughts were harbouring these thoughts, "...and we don't wish to stop in the way of your securing a better position..." It's just the damning sort of way Bruce would say it.

Oh, God, its getting more than I can bear!

June 5th, 1933. Whitsuntide.

I've got 'Minor' back from the Horsforth Garage - all spick and span. They have made an excellent job of her.

I am determined to have one final fling before the fateful day of parting. So I run down to Leicester, in brilliant weather, and we all went picnicking - one day into the heart of "The shire of Shires", to Gumley, which is about seven miles from Market Harborough. I am sure I have seen Parson Dove's Vicarage. (You'll know what I mean, if you have read Whyte- Melville's "Market Harborough"). All through, the weather has been ideal. The next day we went to Hunstanton. Never in my life have I bathed in sea that was warmer. On the way home we had tea beneath the welcome shade of the glorious pines and rhododendrons at Sandringham. I have been on good form, and so have the family. I don't think anyone deserves to be happy who isn't doing something to make other people happy.

All this has been a wonderful change to dreariness of recent Joppa life, and I repeat that I don't care a twopenny damn what happens. For weeks no one seems to have taken any notice of me at all - let alone given me a spot of encouragement.

Its just beginning to dawn on me how irksome, boring and thoroughly unpleasant work can be. The thing to do, apparently, is to do as little as possible for the simple reason there is no reason for doing anything else.

It is pretty obvious that my worthy directors, and in particular Jimmy Bruce think that all young men under the age of 35 or 40 are no bloody good! Life is only liveable because from somewhere within springs the hope that things will turn the corner before long.

But I pray it be soon.

Tuesday, June 27th, 1933.

K.W.6749

This evening I feel sad - I have taken my last leave of 'Minor'. My pocket positively bulges with pound notes - thirty five in all.

An appreciation.

"Minor, my best pal and comfort in moments of joy, and in moments when life has not been altogether a bed of roses. You have been wonderful - always done what has been asked of you, and that has often been much, yet with never a murmur.

Some of my happiest moments have been spent in your company. You have seen my moments of triumph, and you have seen my moments of illusion. You have the key to my passions. And even though we have parted; no money can buy those memories.

God bless you old chap."

July 8th to 23rd, 1933.

"Sables-d'Or-les-Pins".

[Sables-d'Or-les-Pins was, and still is, a beach destination on the coast in the north of Brittany]

I often promised myself a really good holiday, all on my own. At last it has come and this is where I've come to... Sables-d'Or-les-Pins, in Brittany.

This year, more than ever, the need for a 'get-away-from-everything' sort of a holiday has been all the more pressing.

I feel that during the last twelve months I have been standing still, and if that be impossible, then I have slipped back... Nothing in this world can afford to stand still, least of all human energy, and those who won't make an effort to hold what they've got, will soon lose all, and that goes for ideas as well as ducats. I know my energy has somewhat shrunk in the effort to achieve my life's ambition, and I'm sure my creative mind has diminished. There are two things I've learnt of late, the first is to drown my disappointments at Joppa in gallons of beer; and the other is to spend money like water, and I suppose like everything else in the world, all good things have to come to an end sometime or another, and so, this holiday may be called an ending and a beginning.

For some months, I have hardly troubled with Betty. When she was in Yorkshire - I longed for her, and it was a genuine love; but no, she was unrelaxing. So for the last nine months I have settled myself down to a very gay sort of bachelor existence. Therefore imagine my surprise to meet Betty in London, a few days ago - literally "knee-deep". Any wind that might have been in my sails was completely taken away. Then too, since my last entry Dorothy claims mention. Not for one moment that we take each other seriously. I mean we've only seen each other three times. She's a wonderful pal, and a great sport with a dazzling social position, and dizzy wealth. Still, I can see that unless I am extremely careful, I shall be getting myself into a hell of a mess. After all our correspondence (all duly noted) I should have thought Betty was high and dry... Somehow those words are strangely pleasant, reminding me of a loft filled with sunshine, and dried herbs. That is how one ought to feel after a love affair. High and Dry. High above all petty and spiteful feelings, and warm, and sunny, and dry. Like the seasons; love comes and goes, and its the poor and unlucky ones who are left feeling tearful and chilled to the marrow. Low and Damp in fact, instead of feeling high and dry.

Last week I was adamant that I would remain single until I was thirty at least. Now, at Sables-d'Or it is different - to see such charming young married couples. I'll bet none of them are over twenty-eight. They seem so happy. In the men, too, I notice a far-more balanced behaviour, and manner. So all my definite ideas on marriage go where the wind has gone, which went out of my sails in the last paragraph but one!

There is an old saying that if you want a job doing ask a busy man to do it, and you may depend on it. I am slipping into a slipshod way of thought - with comparatively little to think about.

What have I to show for my first year at Joppa? Very little, I have spent much money on having a French tutor. I started with great zest and keenness but this last four or five months there has been a falling off - in not caring whether my home work was done or not; then stifling yawns during instruction. From a linguistic point of view these holidays are hardly a success.

And let me tell you other unpleasant things about myself. I am getting a snob, as I suppose most of us are. I am a hypocrite, as most of us are. And at times I am a liar, as we all are. Still being a snob, I have learnt not to despise them.   Well-bred ones preserve our aristocracy just as varnish preserves old wood.

Evidence for this confession is not far to seek. Glance at my dress. I have been going from strength to strength as it were, in effecting a more and more county and startling style. Perhaps riding has aided and abetted. But ought I not to halt and ponder a few moments on its result with Colin Colins. Didn't Samuel Johnson say:-

"What are acres? What are houses?

146

Only dirt, or wet, or dry.

I am of age, my parents say, Should I?

Scorn their counsel, scorn their pother -
You can hang or drown at last..."

When asked "What colours are your blazer ?" I blasély reply "Wellington" - with an air of condescension. Then again, I make full use of the fact that I have (or rather have had) a car, together with the expression, "Oh, I am with Harold Nickols" to create an impression that demands more than a casual glance. And I make full use of the credit thereby created.

And believe me they are magical words.

I must just mention "Bill's Binge" - the picture of me either dancing with a stuffed animal on top of the piano at 'The Black Bull' at Kettlesing. Or self and "Stormy Weather" crawling about the lounge floor at 'The Hawthorns' barking like dogs at each other, self in her negligé, and she in my bathing costume, and everybody helpless with drunken laughter. We paid the price - the aftermath was dreadful, and for the second time I am seriously considering turning a teetotaller, and being a bachelor for the rest of my earthly days.

Surely the moral to this year is that I must get a little more science into my thinking.

So much for all that.

Sables-d'Or-les-Pins, how can I best describe its charm? Its peacefulness, the blueness of the sky, and the clearness of the sea: Les Patisseries, Berets, Bathing Bridge, Sun-Tan oil, and sand everywhere. Here are some jottings on my last evening, after having enjoyed some ten days of it - sitting on a banc blanc, sur la plage - that is, in front of the derelict Casino, after a wonderful dinner, idly watching the sunset.

I am wonderfully fit, brown, well, and happy, both mentally and physically. This holiday has done me more good than I could have imagined. Its wonderful what the open air will do - plenty of bathing, long walks, Tennis, the sun and the wind, - and good company.

On the whole I got on very well with my French - after I overcame that linguistic shyness, which is characteristic of our race.

I am out here all by myself, and this will be my last evening of peace and quietness for many a long week. During the holiday I have made up my mind on the following points:-

(1) to check all invoices at Joppa, and generally display an untireless and unflagging energy in the office. (Ah, noble soul.).

(2) Stay with a French family next year, and master the language,

(3) Master shorthand,

(4) to realise my ambition - my pleasures must be subordinate to it; that means steadying myself down a little.

(5) Make a success of Rugger this year.

(6) What to say to Mr. Bruce, for instance tell him that criticism can mean both appreciation and depreciation, and at Joppa I get neither. And that being a skipper of a rugger team - a leader of men, I know the full worth of an honest pat on the back just now and again... and a whole lot more.

But I must be going back, the others will be waiting for Bridge.

So much for my last evening. I love the whole place. A score words will suffice for memories. "Tutu, delightful indeed; Enguerrant, Oh! Boy; Yvonne, very nice indeed; Mr. Pennington, Major Davenport, Sinner, Mrs. Gladsden, Peggy and Allen, and Jimmy and Eileen."

Well, oh hell, the last day has come, and we say our goodbyes! We spend a few hours at Dinard, and I am very disappointed. It is often called a millionaires resort, consequently it is half empty. Across the Ranse - par la vedette blanche a Saint Malo, which is as full of character and Dinard is not. There is a dear old Cathedral - very much fingered. *[The ornate, fingered steeple was destroyed during World War Two, and replaced by the much plainer one seen today.]*

To walk round the walls is an education - providing the sun is not too hot. I liked the view from the corner nearest the sea, where you get a good view of Parami. Even Dinard looks well at a distance. Later Dr. & Mrs McKay and self have a wonderfully cheap dinner at "Chez Chuz", or some name very like it, anyway it was good enough for the Queen of Romania. There are a few nightclubs and Bars in the lower quarters, unfortunately our boat sailed at 10pm, and I was unable to offer my morals a delicious risk.

At five a.m. the Steward brings me my tea, and after a shower I get up to watch our progress up the 'Water' - past 'The Needles' which are quite impressive *['The Needles' is a row of three stacks of chalk that rise about 30 metres (98 ft) out of the sea off the western extremity of the Isle of Wight in the English Channel]*, as they breakthrough the morning mist. And gradually leaving The Island of Wight on our right, past the Calshott Seaplane base, we make our way to the docks. We pass 'The Homeric' just returning from a cruise, and I also see 'The Olympic', *['The Homeric' and 'The Olympic' were part of the same Olympic-Class of ships as the better-known 'Titanic']* and the 'Naldera' *[a steam-powered passenger liner owned and operated by the Peninsular and Oriental Steam Navigation Company (P&O) between 1920 and 1938.]*.

At last, we dock - terra-firma again. I manage quite successfully to diddle the Customs, and after an excellent breakfast by The Southern Railway, I am at Waterloo.

I meet Betty, and we lunch on the garden terrace at 'The Savoy' - - Oh, Boy, What Cantaloupe, and Lobster mayonnaise, and Chocolat Gateaux! Again, I repeat, Oh, Boy... and so before many more hours I am back again 'midst the grime and industry of Yorkshire - it all seems like a dream - perhaps it was.

Thursday, August 3rd, 1933.

Had a very pleasant chat with Mr. Noel, in which he imparted some good advice... to keep on, and not get disheartened, and in order to bear up he has added £50 a year to my salary. Three Cheers!

Wednesday, August 9th, 1933.

What marvellous weather we are having. Surely this summer will go down in our History Books as being a return to the 'good old summers'. Ever since July I have been going up to Rawdon Billing for a Picnic Lunch, often with Lewis, to bathe in his dam. Its a treat to get away from the smell, heat, worries, and hustle of Kirkstall Road, for a brief couple of hours in the heat of the day. Just a pleasant dip, and then lunch on the bank - idly watching the birds, or the flowers, or anything. One day a remarkable thing happened. As we lay watching nothing in particular, the hay, which had been newly mown suddenly started 'lifting', then going round in circles, then going straight up in the air to the height of about 40 feet. It was most curious, but never-the-less true. In the evening I have generally changed into my 'shorts', and sandals, and gone for another swim, often at "Newlaithes", they certainly are getting the garden very beautiful, and keeping up the old tradition.

Yesterday, Bill and I went off the "The Tree Arrows" at Borough Bridge, for a splash, then tea on the lawns. The new pool is a great innovation and it has been carried out in very commendable taste. At tea I succeeded to butcher half a dozen wasps with my knife in a raspberry jam tart.

The M.G. went magnificently on the way home.

Before I say adieu, to what has been a tuneful and colourful summer, I must mention tonight. The party consisted of Marjorie, of the Queen's, Burton and Keighley; Bill, mine host and my self. We started by showing Marjorie some of the tit-bits of Yorkshire. Bill knows his Yorkshire well, and we eventually arrive at 'The Red Lion', alias, 'The Red Cat', 'The Pink Pussy', or 'The Kolored Kitten'! at South Stainly, to a dinner that was 'tres soignee' which is the best compliment I can give it. And afterwards liqueurs, Coffee, Cigars, and chocolates in the sunken garden by the lily pond... you know the type, when the cool mellow scent of the evening pervades all and infuses a similar contentedness into ones being.

Saturday, August 20th, 1933.

Have a hell of a cold, probably the result of last weekend at Norbreck, which was positively nauseating. The least said about it the better.

Today, Bill has taken Lewis and self on an M.G. car trial... over parts of Yorkshire that I never knew to exist. In all we went about 60 miles, through Stainburn, Kettlesing, over Ramsgill Moors, through Pateley Bridge, and up Dacre Banks, and back via Leathley. From Dacre Bank top,

I distinctly saw York Minster - a distance of at least thirty miles.

Next spring, when rugger finishes, I must do this on foot, because when travelling mostly between the speeds of 45 and 55 miles per hour, one hasn't many moments to appreciate the wonderful views.

And again today dreams, I would like to spend a week-end at 'The Sportmans Arms', Ramsgill - it looks a wonderful spot - Oh, for a car.

Saturday, August 26th, 1933.

Major Harold Nickols dies after a short illness of 5 days.

I wonder which way the wind will blow now.

Sunday, September 17th, 1933.

- The First Sunday after St. Leger, or, the 14th after Trinity.

This has been a week of considerable trials. Last Thursday,(the 14th), I asked Bruce of his opinion on my joining an evening class - the subject of which was rather high sounding - it being no less than "The British Constitution", and with a sub heading - "Local government and its administration". Unfortunately he took up the wrong attitude altogether, arguing on these lines; that a man cannot serve two masters, either he leaves business and goes in for public work, or he sticks to the former.

He went on to say that some years ago he decided to take up golf, but he found he was being tempted to take an afternoon off now and again, and as he did not feel justified in doing this - he abandoned Golf. Narrow-minded old man - does he expect me to give up rugger? Oh, God!

And when he said, "Well, of course if you are dissatisfied with the Leather Trade, I've nothing more to say. If you think you could better yourself by going in for public work - off you go - with all my good wishes in the world."

The whole affair hurt my inner feeling more than I can say. Of course, it was one of those outwardly trivial little episodes, but, which inwardly one never forgets.

An ambition is shattered.

Another cause for no small amount of anxiety is my decision to plunge into real estate - it will be a hell of a pinch, but, I trust, worth it. Besides it gives one a little wool on ones back so to speak. The question to face during the coming months will be whether to live there or to let it. Both alternatives offer considerable scope.

And still yet another cause for anxiety is my captaincy of The Bohemians, and the enormous amount of work attached to the publicity side, and Entertainments Committee; still I suppose much of it can be done in the 'firms' time!

As I survey this week I think the moral of it is to try and lead as balanced sort of life as is possible in this chaotic little niche of mine.

Thursday, September 21st, 1933.

The last ten days have kept me devilishly busy. Messrs. Barkley, Blockey and Bottomley are all away holidaying, and young Bailey from the Warehouse is ill. Yesterday, I was just about up to my neck, when Bruce came up to me and announced that it was time that I started travelling. So tomorrow, I am to take the Talbot (the works Car), and try my luck in Huddersfield. It was very sudden, but I was ready for the opportunity. Damn it - have I not been waiting patiently for over twelve months for it to come my way?

The enormous nerve strain involved in starting up from cold, to my pitch of vivacity when doing my sales stuff - left me almost a little frightened. Added to which is the responsibility of quoting prices, especially when Bruce never tells you anything (or anyone else for that matter). You have simply every damned thing to find out for yourself.

It is by no means easy to rub up at five minutes notice, all the witty retorts that are part of a salesman's stock-in-trade.

I make a resolution. Never give Bruce any rest... keep firing questions at him. I must get a goodly string ready for him this weekend.

Saturday, September 24th, 1933.

This afternoon I have had my first experience as Skipper of the Bohemians... no little ordeal, but by gad worth it!

As Tommy Hewison said to me in his letter "... for my dear Tim, the heart of an "A" team captain knows more sorrows than the joys of life, but it was an experience I found well worth while..."

This afternoon we were playing The Old Hymerians at Hull, and we travelled three men light - a bad enough handicap in all conscience. But all the lads played a sterling game, and only lost by 18 points to 5. And I have the satisfaction of knowing that I made a roaring success of it. Can I ever forget the train journey back to Leeds? Everyone 'nicely', and joining in a stentorian and lewd lament, all the way home.

Wednesday, September 27th, 1933.

Tom Barkley, in the Office and self have decided that it would be rather a good idea if we had a little annual dinner to commemorate our beginnings at Joppa - this year has been a bit of a struggle, but more or less enjoyable. Who knows what the future will hold now that Mr. Harold is no more, and so it was in this frame of mind that we decided on the Queens.

After a couple of 'shorts' we had a medium dinner in the Grill which we washed down suitably with a bottle of 1923 Bollinger. He would persist, poor boy, in telling very lewd tales, and not in very good taste, as the poor boy doesn't know how to whisper. But then the fellow's never been brought up.

I drank a silent toast "...Here's to the hope that further prosperity and advancement will favour us both before our next dinner."

On the whole it was an amusing evening.

October, 11th, 1933. *[Wednesday]*

For some reason my journey up to London to The Leather Fair has been wonderfully refreshing. There is a peculiar charm about the lather trade - as I said last year.

The Fair a couple of years ago was a brilliant affair, when I managed the whole of our stand single handed, then last year was pretty feeble, for I was very small beer on the Joppa stand, and now this year I am getting to know more of the folk that call for "the odd'n", for which the stand of Harold Nickols is famed throughout the Leather Trade.

I know not the reason for my elation. Perhaps it was this, and perhaps that; perhaps because of my relative closer companionship to Mr. Bruce, or, perhaps because I stayed at The Midland Grand.

Perhaps because, I've had so many stupid little compliments thrown at me - so much so in fact - I am almost beginning to think myself a 100% guy! Some wise old boy once said that it was easier to uproot a mountain with a needle, than to remove pride from the heart of man. And by gad how true it is of life!

Perhaps, it was because Dad came up to The Fair, or, that I introduced myself to F.H. Briggs.

Or, was it I wonder because I saw Tim Mux[worthy], or because I achieved fame by having a third helping at Simpsons, or that educational pup crawl to Bloomsbury with Harry G. Modern art. Phew! We finished up in Mayfair at The Running Horse - a delightful little pub, horribly full, where London's "Bright young things" quaff their pints.

Thursday, October 19th, 1933.

I feel like writing quite a lot tonight.

My brain feels surprising clear after last nights debauche. Leslie Mason's party at "The Drovers Arms", Bishop Thornton. I took Jean, and Bill took Joan Bains. Bill kindly offered me hospitality at "The Hawthorns", which needless to say was accepted, and thither I make my way.

After a leisurely bath, and donning my dinner kit, and an excellent dinner, we set sail. We dropped anchor at both The Majestic and The Grand in Harrogate, and we were in rare fettle when we arrived at "The Drovers".

We were just in nice time to take our parts as 'extras' in Leslie's Film, which as you may have guessed is the excuse for the party. After a midnight ham and egg supper it became an orgie - in a sudden burst of sound, the result of refreshments, each began to shout, sing, and dance, or anything else he wished, and went as far as he judged suitable - Imagine the chaos. Poor old Duncan must have got pretty tight, as he took the wrong turning on the way home. Whilst it would be both unkind and unfair to say the car got out of control, but, when rounding a bend, the car - for some unaccountable reason overturned. The picture of four very tight people climbing out through the sunshine roof and tramping some three miles back to The Drovers on a damned cold night strikes me as being oddly funny.

The others, including myself finished off the evening, at Harold Mason's new mansion in North Lane. I couldn't help wondering who they had to decorate the place, for it does them great credit.

I turned out the light at three fifteen.

These jocose evenings are all very well and whilst they are pleasant and gay, but they don't get you anywhere. I'm sure they are not too good for my soul and I'm still more sure that they are worse for my pocket. For these last three months I have been living at the rate of some £3 a week on piffling amusements. And its so bloody hard to say "no"! Dear old Bill sets a lively pace, and matters are not improved by the fact that a very busy and expensive season lies ahead. Being captain of a Rugger XV isn't an exactly economical position.

A couple of years ago I couldn't have believed myself capable of such a weakening. My living expenses have reached an exorbitant figure, and it is becoming increasingly difficult to live within my means. My promotion in salary does not seem to have made the slightest difference to that ghastly pile of bills.

Then on top of it all is my venture in real estate... the purchase of "Woodbottom Lawn" and, 'ere long will come the decision whether to live in it, or let it. There are so many points to be borne in mind that I am torn with indecision. By living alone would give rise for much idle speculation - and not all of it too friendly like. There is the servant problem, and expense thereof.

One thing I know, that living by myself, I should want everything neat. I have always despised people who pretend that inexpensive things are just as good as if not better than luxuries. I'm afraid my idea of 'neatness' would have rather disastrous financial results.

I rather fear my friends. A single and eligible young man with a charming house, would almost sure to be made a convenience of, and this would, of course, be very undesirable.

Another problem would be how to escape from "Woodbottom" in a magnanimous, yet decisive manner. For it must only be done leaving nothing but the warmest of feelings behind. To leave with any regret on either side would be little short of disastrous.

I think the desire for solitude is common to all of us at times, but how would it stand the test of time? Living by oneself, one would certainly develop a sense of responsibility, but will not answer for other directions. I should certainly have to overcome certain personal difficulties, and what of the domestic side.

To borrow Duncan's expression, I should have to pipe down, and lead a more piped existence. From an investment point of view I think it is sound, for it is a bonny little property - facing the sun.

The other night I had a long talk with Bruce on the question of property as an investment. He expressed pleasure that my mind was running on those lines, and agreed whole-heartedly. I was then given a short catechism on the short comings of modern youth and the rising generation - his favourite topic.

Apropos Betty. By jove I caught socks last week, when I dined with my illustrious Aunt Edith, and unloaded my heavy heart. She expressed herself very strongly, and intimated that I had her blessings 'en avance', if I was rash enough to get engaged.

Here are what will probably be the last letters that will ever pass between Betty and myself and that being so:-

(17.x.33.)

My dear Betty,

The usual apologies for not writing, but as you say its my turn; here goes.

I was disappointed at not seeing you at The Leather Fair. But I know you said that you'd be extra busy in getting Sir A. S-M off to Canada. It would have done us good to have continued our chat - after we had both slept on it.

Let me be as concise as possible on a matter which it is horribly difficult to be brief upon. But here is a dreadful confession.

Three years ago, I loved you, tremendously. Then you went to London, and, gradually, very gradually I slipped away. But let it be quite clearly understood that it was through no fault of my own. Three-quarters of my time was spent working pretty hard. Then what comes next? Rugger, my French classes, or the friendships of Duncan, Bill and Lewis, for we have certainly had wonderful times together: Swimming, Golfing, Tennis, Walking, or playing Bridge... so these last two years life has on the whole run a very pleasant course.

Anyway the point is this: I think it would be best if I definitely said that I have absolutely no intentions, other than our friendship.

I know that, hereafter you'll always associate my name with mud. I apologise, and hope that when you come to Leeds, that it will not mean that you will refuse to see me altogether, and absolutely.

Ever,

Betty's reply came by return of post, almost.

My dear Timothy,

Many thanks for your letter of 18.x.33.

I am so glad that you have at last been quite frank with me - I think a thousand times more of you than I should have done if you had let things drift on in the same old way. Now we know what we are all playing at, so to speak.

Of course, I shall only be too pleased to see you when I am in Leeds - surely we can go on being good friends - as a matter of fact, I am coming up in about a weeks time. I have got a temporary job. I won't tell you any more, so that if you don't want to see me you need not, and I shall quite understand. But don't say I wont see you - because I will. And another thing I don't think any worse of you for first telling me how you feel, but much more.

I think perhaps I will send you my address later - that is if you really want it, and I will let you have it.

All the best for you -

P.S. This all seems rather feeble, but I have known how things were for nearly two years - only I was too afraid of hurting you to say anything.

Tuesday, November 7th, 1933.

Duncan and I have definitely decided on a drastic economy campaign, and in dead earnest.

Sunday, November 12th, 1933.

Yesterday, was my first experience of skippering my team to victory, we were playing Headingley Old Boys and we won 5-3. The chaps played a great game - tackling hard and low. The long run of defeats have taught me one thing, and that is to lose like a sportsman.

Another Armistice has come and gone, I spent this year's Silence in the least dramatic way imaginable, for I stood with Mr. Blockey at the gates at Joppa, and watched all the traffic come to an absolute standstill, it was certainly more impressive than being in an office or warehouse. Next year, if possible, I would like to spend it as far away from anyone as possible - alone on the moors, in the middle of a field, or at the top of one of the big trees in the woods.

The events of today, however, have impressed me far more than the slightly superficial proceedings of yesterday.

I went with Grannie to the Remembrance Service at Guiseley Church, and incidentally today, is the first Sabbath that the plaque has been up to the memory of Uncle Walter.

It was an ideal November's day, with the last leaves of summer turning to a deeper and richer brown, giving a very vivid contrast to the greenness of the fields, and the blueness of the sky, whilst the crispness of the day made it feel good to be alive. And it is on days like today that I begin to realise my appreciation for what those chaps gave, when they went out to France, and died without a whimper. By the remembrance of their dauntlessness, I feel I can brace myself to many a hard task involving pain or suffering, by asking myself if my manhood were so weak as to give way.

I admire Canon Howson tremendously, and his sermon was brilliant. He frankly admitted that soldiers and soldiering always had, and always will have a certain glamour for him, and for most of us for that matter - citing the thrill it gave every Briton when he watched the changing of the Guard at Buckingham Palace - when the band crashes into a splendid marching tune… and the men - what fine examples of manhood, carrying out their ceremonial as one man. He went on to say that extensive disarmament by any one nation was futile - only making the aggressors task more simple. In other words it would be like sending the lamb to the slaughter. There would still be war even if there were no arms. In the American Civil War, at the outset, neither side had arms of any description. The one essential for peace was a will for peace - which, he would not be rash enough to say was an easy thing to attain, and having attained… to keep up. Because here comes one of the difficulties - who is not tremendously proud that he is an Englishman? There is no plainer language than Nationalism.

He reminded us that the young German of today was just the same as the young British man - they remembered precious little of the War - No nation as powerful as the Teutons could stay depressed forever.

He also stressed the futility of further War - it meant the complete annihilation of a generation.

And also the absurdity of an International Army. Who, he asked would serve in its ranks, and who would command it - unless the pay were excessively high.

If this country does not make full use of its freedom... its heritage by patriotic readiness, its destiny needs no divination. Its freedom will vanish soon, and history will not greatly regret it.

The whole show left a deep impression in my mind. After the service, Aunt Louie and I went for a walk through the fields by the Rectory. It was great, and I couldn't help wondering what might have been - had we not won the War.

Thursday, November 23rd, 1933.

Oh, happy me! Last night was brilliant, and its occasion was my Toast Mastering at The Leeds Round Table Charter Night Dinner at The Metropole at which 138 sat down to an excellent dinner, the 139th, I regret I didn't enjoy the dinner a little bit, a bad case of stage fright.

Oh, Boy. But afterwards I think I was congratulated by everyone excepting, of course, The Lord Mayor. Even Cousin Harold condescended to approve, so I must have done well.

What is there to be said in the speeches? Dick Walker's and Allan Beaumont's were certainly the highlights of the evening. Allan's material and delivery were 'the goods'. Whilst Dick's command of manner, and easy wit charmed everyone.

Tonight I have received a topping letter from Edmund Wood, expressing his appreciation of my efforts in a very delicate way.

Saturday, November 27th, 1933.

I was skipper of our "A" against Roundhay "B" and won by 20 points to nil, felt a bit jaded in the evening, otherwise I should have gone out with the lads and made whoopee.

Grannie has purchased a wireless, the evening passed quite pleasantly.

Monday, November 27th, 1933.

Feel a different man this morning.

Possibly that at last - at long last. I am to visit the Eastern Counties this week. Glory be to God!

Yesterday, too, put me in fine fettle. I went riding with John Holdsworth - a pleasant little hack as far as the Stanhope Arms for the odd Sunday morning jar. Later in the paddock I negotiated all the jumps successfully, and in no small spectacular manner, generally speaking I felt as proud as hell.

The afternoon was both amusing and pleasant. Duncan and I, as is our wont, went to coffee at The Hawthorns, and were introduced to Barbara Burnett - a friend of Mrs Irwin's from Jersey. She is a great sport. Later we went to visit my property in Horsforth.

The fun was fast and furious, I can just imagine my neighbours expostulating, "...the young Mr. Thackray isn't even in residence yet - what on earth will it be like when he is?"

What priceless chance for dear old Mrs. Grundy. Practically the first glimpse they get of the new owner is that of him with two of his friends and a smart young lady climbing up a ladder and through a bedroom window.

The caretaker Johnny who had the key was nowhere to be found, and this was the only way of gaining entry. The scene which was us shifting the kitchen cabinet, must have surpassed even the inimitable George Clarke *[George Broome Clarke (11 April 1886 – 21 December 1946) was an English comedian, best known in the 1930s for his sketch "My First Car".]*. My sides ached with laughing.

And so home to a typical winter's tea... piles of piping hot muffins and picklets. Then we settled down to a comfortable twilight with Radio Luxembourg and idle chatter, and as befits a Sunday evening - I settled down with "The Tatler", and "Sporting Dramatic", and digested the current number of "Country Life" and such an occupation never fails to please me. In it there was an article review on Whyte Melville's "Riding Recollections", of which I have just got a copy, extraordinarily interesting.

He must have been a marvellous type of English country gentleman - true, every inch of him to traditional type. I must keep a weather eye for any biographies of him.

The third thing that pleases me is that I think that I have discovered one way of dealing with Mr. Noel Nickels. When he starts his questionnaire bombardment - answer as concisely as possible, and turn the answer into a question thereby getting him to do the talking. If you succeed you'll be damned clever.

Friday, December 1st, 1933.

And what of my first visit to The Eastern Counties? Its grand to be 'out' again so to speak - though from a business point of view it would hardly set the Thames on fire.

I made some notes on Ely Cathedral, but have misplaced them. When you've walked the maize just as you go in; you will have done the equivalent of mounting the steps of the tower, and, believe me its far easier. The building as a whole was very interesting as it is said to be one of the best examples of the transitional period of Norman to early English architecture.

December 16th, 1933. *[Saturday]*

Today, and one cannot help but review it with certain misgiving, but lets put it down to youthful exuberance. I admit to being a silly young ass, I went out with some of my friends - the Dash and Crash Brigade, and got gloriously tight, so tight that we got silly - pinching public time tables, wrenching them clean from their moorings, but this was small fry to the general havoc we created at White Cross. My new check coat, which Duncan describes as "...another of Tim's startling ensembles." - personally I think "Voyant" - quite sufficient.

Whatever its description, it was my downfall, as a Robert *[Robert Peel - Police Officer]* copped me - the others being dressed as normal citizens - escaped. They took my name and address, to which I obliged in the orthodox Public School code. Then they wanted the names of my associates, which I politely refused - saying that if there was any trouble I would rather shoulder it, than drag my friends into the mess. All this seemed to create quite a sound impression and I don't think there will be any consequences.

But talking of clothes; it really amused me to see everyone look at me as though I were Exhibit "A" in a murder trial - when I was sandwiched between two great bobbies.

Christmas 1933. December 27th. *[Wednesday]*

I wonder if I am getting very boorish, because the domestic side of Christmas 1933 has hardly been enjoyable. It may be that I get so well looked after at Woodbottom that such firm domesticities such as washing-up, peeling spuds, setting tables, and cleaning that disagreeable and digesting aftermath that each meal is bound to leave, never for one moment enter my head. I can be cheerful under most conditions, but when it comes to being cheerful in a household that for over twelve months has been servant-less, it is beyond me. Yesterday, I made a pact with myself never to spend another Christmas at Braybrooke - under similar conditions.

Mother was definitely not on form. Fagged after all the extra work that Christmas brings (and we are a dreadful family for food), and when she's in that state she sometimes lacks balance when there's anything in the house, and that makes everything extremely difficult. All this reacts on the old man, and he becomes more awkward in the house, and he is so stupid.

One cannot help but admire his dogged courage, or is it mere stupidity? After all the family's gone through - lost all our money - our position - sold a good deal of our furniture - and a whole heap more, and he still keeps so blitheringly cheerful. It beats me!

Fancy having to get up at the ungodly hour of six-thirty; light the fire, get his own breakfast - under very doubtful conditions, because he has simply no idea of making anything look appetising. Then to a day's work, which, to hear him talk is many times worse than mine, then home to washing up.

I very strongly disapprove, they've plenty of money to keep a maid and live a little more civilised life. I've come to the conclusion that it must be for outward show.

Just before I left Joppa, I had another row with young Teddy Bailey. My contention, (and a very just one, too) was that insufficient work was being done in the warehouse. The cheeky young swine had the blasted nerve to turn round and tell me that when I got a bit older I should probably learn more sense. It would have given me the greatest joy to have told him to put on his coat and clear out of the place. As it was, I suffered the insult. To have done otherwise would have probably queered the pitch with Mr. Bruce, because the Bailey family are Bruce's pets. Open rupture must be avoided at all costs, it is quite likely that within five years, young Bill Bailey (Teddy's brother) will have control of the warehouse, so you see the folly of it? In a certain class of uneducated mind foresight is often interpreted as guilty knowledge.

This Christmas everyone in the office got a silk handkerchief from Bruce - excepting me, and Tom Barklay actually got a Turkey. I wonder by the way if I am acting with discretion suitable to my years by taking him to Polly's for the odd jar, and by generally treating him as an equal.

All this unhappiness always makes people look so stupid. I'm not joking, I'm perfectly sure it does.

Before I leave, the family let me give vent to another displeasure - when I presented the old man with his Christmas prize - a Dunhill Tobacco pouch, he didn't accept very graciously, and when I asked him to accept the Turkey, as they did last year, he was positively nasty.

It is not, therefore, very remarkable to relate, that, on my way home, I did a bit of thinking, coming to some conclusions, and finally arriving at one or two decisions, namely:-

1. To try and be more appreciative of Grannie's efforts on my behalf.

2. That I shall have to go easy for a while. At the moment I must be in debt to the tune of some £40 *[Equivalent to £3,300 in 2023]*. It has always been one of my maxims to keep one's book debts down to an equivalent of a month's salary. Of course, taking the long view, my assets far

outweigh my liabilities. My one determination at the moment is to have sufficient surplus to repay the £15 Bill lent me for the conveyance, and completion of "Woodbottom Lawn", in May last. I must not, and will not, let him down.

Every cloud has a brighter side. We will forget the above - or try to. For weeks, now, I have been looking forward to seeing dear old Tim's face again - though to miss by a short head the realisation of one of my ambitions was very hard cheese.

Boxing Day, when some go to the town; some to the country; some take the rail; some their motors; some their families; and some only themselves. But the rural and often the suburban population generally incline to a hunt. They are not very particular as to style, so long as there are a certain number of hounds, and some men in scarlet, to blow their horns, halloo and crack their whips.

Sadly to relate, we neither rode 'with' the hounds, nor 'to' the hounds. We arrived at Brown's farm on the dot of nine, and within fifteen minutes we had mounted our redoubtable hacks, and made short work of my flask of Sherry to keep out the cold, and started our eleven mile hack to Hinkley, the (theoretical) meet of The South Atherstone. We did the eleven miles with quippings, and with expectations that were only of the highest.

Quietly - I think old Brown played us one of his horsey tricks on us!! For we trotted into Hinkley Market Place as the clock on the Co-operative Stores boomed the hour of eleven - but neither man nor beast, nor fox nor hound was to be seen. We learned at the local pub that the meet was at Market Bosworth - some five miles further on. So, Onward Christian Soldiers... with liberal refreshment at all the pubs.

We cantered up country lanes, and trotted down bridle paths. The local rustics did their best to be helpful, saying, "...Oh, close by," when asked the direction of hounds. And this as most hack hunters will well know to their cost is generally anything but "Close by" - nor was it so on this occasion. At any rate we were very near the running - judging by the number of cars and people we saw - I believe they thought we were The South Atherstone Hunt itself - little wonder if they happened to have seen Tim's badly fitting stock, or my unorthodox hat. The whole show was a scream.

Our only consolation was that had we found hounds - hunting would have been out of the question as visibility was no more than 25 yards.

As is customary for men who are admirers of horse-flesh, and live by the fox - we again refreshed. I can remember 9 glasses of ale, 2 Ginger Brandies, 2 Rums, and 3 Brandies, then I got as foggy as the weather. But I learned that it is highly satisfying to both body and soul to be astride a horse complete with cigar, and jolly good company.

We returned to tea in front of a colossal fire at The Bell Hotel, where I dozed off lying full length on the couch, tired, very tired, but very much at peace with the world.

Thursday, January 4th, 1934.

I feel better for two reasons, the first is that I have let "Woodbottom Lawn" for 11/6d per week, which leaves me a balance of about £2 over and above my payments to The Building Society, to cover cost of painting etc. My tenant is Mrs. Hannah Marsden, who I expect (and hope) will be there for life, and the other reason is that it has made me make up my mind on the problem of ever living there myself - though at the cost of my independence - so long cherished.

Monday, January 15th, 1934.

The flutter that Dorothy caused within my breast some six months ago, is unfortunately fluttering away.

I hope I don't become one of the mob - that gets a girl, engaged, then married, just because it is the correct thing to do, and because he's frightened of being called subnormal by his friends. My definition of a bachelor is one of those wise men who never make the same mistake once.

I went riding yesterday, but it was very tame, as compared with Leicester, but nevertheless provided welcome exercise.

I have decided to give up my French classes, because I get no encouragement, and because I cannot afford another five guineas.

Rugger, is my saving grace. It is tremendous fun being the skipper - having command over my fellows, and I enjoy writing the reports for the press each week. It is both good experience and good practice. The only snag is that it is hardly an economical hobby.

At Joppa, this year has opened as pleasantly as last year departed, perhaps I am learning after all where my bread is buttered. And my worries more imaginary than real.

January 16th, 1934. *[Tuesday]*

I visit a Coal Mine.

The owners of the pit are The Flocton Coal Co. Ltd., and the mine was The Hartley Bank Colliery, Notherton, which is quite near Horbury. I was excited all day, in the anticipation of such adventure.

We arrived at the Colliery about seven, on a very dark, cold, windy, rainy, and in short a typical winter's night. After undressing in the colliery's communal changing rooms, each of us were served out with a miner's lamp. Quite heavy, they are, weighing I should judge about a pound and a half. They are electric - the juice coming from a small accumulator, which will last for about twelve hours.

We were then shown all over the working above ground - the air changing machinery - the winding gear - the water pumps - the boilers - the steam turbines, generating current at some 3,000 revs per minute. The Hartley Mains Colliery is an "All-electric" mine, and is considered 'completely safe', they have not had a fatality within the last ten years, which was good enough for me.

And now for the Big Thrill! The cage; eight of us squeeze in. The doors are clanged together. The "alright" is given... and off we go, exactly 234 yards in, as near as I could judge, about twenty seconds. If we had been miners proper, it would be 7 1/2 hours before we should see daylight again, or as they call it "7 1/2 from bank to bank". My first impression, on stepping out of the cage, was to be acutely aware of a buzzing in my ears, due to the rarefied atmosphere and feel a draught - somewhere near gale force. The place was spacious, clean, and well lighted.

We were then conducted to a small office, where we were searched, and our lamps checked over. Instead of using pit ponies for conveying the coal from the face to the pit bottom, they use the endless rope system, complete with many safety gadgets. Each truck will carry about 7 or 8 hundredweights.

The foreman laddie explained the various strata's to us. The Hartley Mains Colliery has two workable seams of coal; the Silkston, or The New Hards seam, which gives a moderate House coal, and is about 20 to 24 inches wide, the other an extremely good manufacturing steam coal, this is called the Wheatley Hill seam, and is deeper by about four inches.

The intricacies of the return air shafts are very well thought and carried out. We then start our hike to the coal face, where the coal cutters are in operation... a distance of about three quarters of a mile.

Along the main galleries there was no difficulty in walking upright, but for the last 400 yards we had to crawl... almost on all-fours.

As we approached the coal face, it became appreciably hotter. It is interesting to know that every 50 feet you descend into the bowels of the earth becomes one degree hotter. At last we came to where the chaps were at work. The actual working distance is a "200 yard-face" and the coal cutter cuts in a depth of 4'6" each cut. The cutter does not actually cut the coal as you would have expected - but just underneath the seam proper. These men, five of them to a gang, are paid by the foot (of coal cut). The colliers - that is, the actual hewers of coal are paid by his individual coal output. A collier can earn anything from 15/- to 25/- a shift, and, damnit they deserve it. Though I am perfectly sure sympathy is wasted.

We did the job thoroughly, as we crawled in, and lay long-side the miners. One couldn't help but notice (nay almost feel), the wonderful sense of comradeship that is abroad in the mine, but is it to be wondered at? The dust made by the cutters was hardly credible. The next job was that of mining my chunk of coal, necessitating lying in a most awkward position, on my side with a pick. Of course, I got my eyes full of dust, and I bumped my elbows, but that is only to be expected with the uninitiated.

Our short fraternity with the miners soon came to an end, but not until we had exchanged a cheery "Cheerio", and discussed the prospects of Leeds United with all the fellows. And so we return to the bank top. Our lamps are handed back, and we return to our clean clothes, after a dip in the Communal baths - great fun.

Mr. Elliot, the Manager, then regaled us with ale, and my word it tasted good.

Three Cheers - long, loud, and lusty.

Wednesday, January 24th, 1934.

Last night, I went to hear our Prime Minister, Mr. Ramsay Macdonald at a mass political meeting, in The Town Hall at Leeds.

To my mind, the exhibition of "booing" and jeering by the labour toughs was very regrettable, for, after all he is the first minister in the land - be it for good or bad. He must be a pretty able man to have got to the top of the ladder. To be in perpetual opposition is a bad school of thought. The wary politicians of our Government, who push themselves into office by this means - take great care to govern by rules entirely opposed to those they formally expounded. You need not go to China to see that - in fact there is no need to go further than The Leeds Town Hall tonight...

Actually I don't think he was on very good form. He couldn't help but sense the general feeling in the room. That of toleration, and not that of wild enthusiasm. His loquations were more in the nature of an appeal - towards the heart, rather than the head.

This method will doubtless bring in the votes, and secure his seat in the House. Some of his appeals, however, were hardly sound business propositions. He talked a good deal about rationalisation and nationalisation and all sorts of other "...ations".

This morning we had Councillor W. L. Haley in the office at Joppa, and the usual combat started. Personally I would like to know what the necessary qualifications are to give away other folks money. He openly admitted that he gave the maximum allowed by law to the man who applied for Public Assistance, who had five or six kids. Its a downright scandal.

I nearly boiled-over (inwardly) when he started about the insufficiency of a forty shillings a day personal allowance, when on deputations in London.

Afterwards the discussion drifted on to the new Socialistic scheme in the Leeds slum clearance... for rent-free council Houses. This would create yet another expensive public department.

These rent-free dwellers, would soon adopt an illegal sentiment attitude towards a life of luxury - beyond all dreams of even Mr. Ramsay Macdonald.

The scheme if it comes into force, will aid and abet thriftlessness, dishonesty, and discontent, and generally demoralise the working class, and the final result will be the loss of that precious thing we call character.

I'm sure the country is going to the dogs.

Monday, February 26th, 1934.

A month has slipped away - pleasantly enough - since my last entry. But really nothing seems to happen to breathe monotony of the daily round. Its just Joppa from nine in the morning until six, and from then onwards either at The Vesper, Training or dominoes, or Round Table, or visiting or dining out with one of my many friends, invariably good entertainment. But the best of the bunch, however, is by my own fireside at Woodbottom.

The fear that I am losing some of my self-confidence is gradually taking hold, and with no set job at Joppa, I am getting tangled in its petty jealousies. I don't complain too bitterly; why should I? I can do pretty well as I like, for instance, I am writing these notes in the firm's time. Work in connection with both Round Table and The Bohemians all comes from the same spring. Last week I even borrowed the Talbot, the works car, to go to a dance at The Road House. That staggered everybody I can tell you.

But as against these comparative assets, there are the eccentricities of Mr. Bruce, probably due to senile decay, but it is very trying. I'm never sure as to whether he approves or disapproves. I have been made to feel junior for so long that I almost feel j'en suis un *[Translation - I am one]*. You know they've no sort of personnel policy at Joppa; no sort of recruiting policy - by promotion and the training of personnel generally. Points which are regarded as absolutely essential to The Army, Navy, or Air Force, and the Civil Service. My opinion regarding Chrome sides has been entirely ignored and the turn-over is poorer by some £10,000. *[Over £800,000 in 2023]*

Today, when H. Hall of York called, and the three of us were in the private office. Bruce deliberately sent me into the warehouse on some petty fogging errand, as if to get rid of me purposely.

Such occurrences as these only go to sharpen my curiosity - hence my nickname... Mr. N. Parker. Last week I suggested another visit to The Eastern Counties but Bruce only poured cold water on the idea. He seems to have taken Huddersfield away with the other hand. It's pretty disheartening; perhaps I am too sensitive to life's rebuffs.

My latest madness is the project of joining the Royal Air Force Reserve. I can do most things, and if I thought I could escape from Joppa for the requisite period of training of six or seven weeks, without imperilling my job I'd go like a shot. One mustn't pull the string so hard that it breaks.

In a fit of misguided heroic, I have joined the panel of the Leeds blood transfusion donors - this is in pursuance of The Round Table tennets "Service before Self". I suppose it all comes in the science of citizenship.

Arthur Bell has offered me the Secretaryship of The Bohemians next season, and I shall probably take it on.

The worst aspect of all this inharmony at Joppa is that it brings you down to its own level, and I become irritable at Woodbottom. At the moment open Warfare exists between Ogre and myself. At times he is impossible. This morning Grannie said to me at breakfast that I seriously ought to be seriously on the look-out for a wife. My reply was "God forbid"! I can imagine nothing more ghastly than the contemplation of matrimony. Which reminds me that I wrote to Betty at Christmas, and since then complete silence, and I am very sorry.

My finance is slowly recovering, though I'm afraid my little venture as a property owner will hold me pretty tight this summer. I haven't the faintest notion as to where my holiday money is coming from.

I wonder what the future will say as to the wisdom or folly of such a deal. Will the effort be worth it?

Saturday, March 24th, 1934.

Hear the skylark for the first time this year. We were playing rugger at West Park, against Old Modernians. It was not a particularly hard game, but enjoyed it immensely. All my chaps played like heroes. The backs were definitely weak, but it was a weakness that is the result of inexperience rather than incompetence.

April Fool's day. EASTER, 1934

Or The field was comprised of...

I have always said that holidays are wretchedly unsettling sorts of things; and so they are. I suspect that it is due to the comparison of leisure to the canker that comes of the drabness of the Joppa routine.

Well chaps, - one of my most cherished ambitions has at long last been achieved. I am at long last a fox hunter.

Last Thursday, after Joppa, I went to The Red House, Scarborough. Mrs. Mead never alters - always having the same old plateful of domestic troubles, and, whilst it is entertaining for anything from a few days to a fortnight; practically speaking it would be an impossibility to live there. You see at once, my dear Watson, the trend of my thoughts. It would be foolish to jeopardise any chances that may or may not exist in that direction.

Mrs M has very generously subsidised my riding to the tune of seventy bob, so I have done myself proud, and had a horse each morning... and yesterday the grand finale... a day with the Staintondale.

I had hoped that I should have gone with young Tom Shaw, but, no the old man took me. The hounds met at Lindhead beck, some five miles out towards Claughton. Old Tom duly lighted his cigar, and we were well underway by 10.30. 'Ere long we were joined by other sportsmen, and so to the meet. I was extremely shy and self-conscious, firstly that I should be capped, and, secondly that I was so conspicuous in my foul green hat, instead of an orthodox bowler. The weather from a riders point of view was exhilarating; but from a hunter's rotten. It was clear, bright, and sunny, with a strong north-easter blowing.

The field comprised of about thirty-five mounted followers, or as the 'Scarborough Mercury' sportingly puts it "...and a capital muster of real sporters congregated". The hounds moved off towards the sea, and were taken to the Stour hills, and then to the quarries, we took up our position on the high ground to the left. A fox was soon up and went across the open into the big wood, where unfortunately he got safely to ground. Then a long, long trail to find another. There was nothing to be found in the big wood. Then to Standing Stones Moor, Hartoft Slack, Stubbs Low Moor, and several small spinneys, then on to Knagg's Whin, and Cowgarth Slack, but never a fox.

I cannot say that I was very impressed with moorland hunting, and I sampled a good deal in the afternoon. About four Tom signalled, and we decided it was time to be retracing our steps, and so we turned our horses after pleasant "Good Night"'s to the rest of the field. And after equally pleasant exchanges with sundry road menders, farm hands, etc, returning from the fields, we reach the outskirts of Scarborough.

All told I was just over seven hours in the saddle - and, no trace of stiffness.

- Only to have a small settled income, and a small farm estate - a couple of Hunters and... Ah well, such are only for the chosen few, and not for the likes of me.

But I ask for nothing more.

Sunday, April 22nd, 1934.

Saw swallows for the first time this year, walking with Duncan at Apperley Bridge.

Monday, April 23rd, 1934.

Am getting very windy re next weeks Steeple Chase, or as the lads call it 'Pint to Pint' in London. Expect I shall get a ticking off from Leicester, which, on the whole will be justified, as I ought not to afford it.

Sunday, April 29th, 1934.

"...Tremendous Ales, Colossal Weirds,

Crashing Cads and Tous jours la politeese..." *[Translation: Everyday politeness]*

Friday's mixture of intense nervous excitement at the prospect of yesterday made both work and the thought of food out of the question. Father met the train at Leicester and to my utter amazement did not tick me off, in fact everything was the reverse, and we all had a very pleasant evening - as Grannie would say '...in the bosom of my family'. Yesterday's train journey to London was spoilt by its running an hour late and being filled with a particularly vulgar type of Cup Final crowd. Leigh was waiting at St. Pancras to meet me. We went straight up to his digs, where we changed and had a rapid sandwich luncheon. We had barely finished when Gordon K. called to take us to the Stables, or in plainer words to Mr. Drage's dirty little farm. I don't pretend to be a judge of horseflesh in any way, but I'm jolly sure that mine was a 'nappy brute. My judgement soon turned out to be nearer the truth than I had imagined.

Imagine my horror when I saw the 'oss being bridled with a new double curb snaffle, complete with martingale. Expostulation would have been worse than useless, and besides old Drage had nothing else.

My adventures were not long in beginning, as we had rather an unpleasant encounter with a couple of buses and some white railings on the way up to the course.

However we arrived without further incident. Where about 150 sporters had gathered. Further adventures were not long in coming my way. It happened on the way down to the farm, when we were inspecting the course. In full view of everybody the 'ugly brute' started a particularly vicious bout of rearing and plunging - so vicious in fact that it came right over, or as near as the martingale would let it, then fell, or slipped, sideways. I regret to say that I became unput, and the brute bolted. Altogether it was a horribly embarrassing and nerve shattering situation.

There were two races; the Club Race, and the Open Race, and I not being an honoured member of the former had to take my luck in the latter. During the Club Race I was too busily occupied in fixing my spurs, and too crestfallen to take an intelligent interest. Tim Muxworthy won in flying style. And now for my turn. The Steward fixes my number on my back, and the Bookie is offering fantastic odds on "The Gentleman from the North". We are directed to the starting post then at last... would he never drop his flag?... We're off...

Leigh told me afterwards what a fine sight it looked eight riders going the first half mile:

"Hell for leather
Altogether..."

And, indeed very fine it was until the second jump. But with the new reins getting well wet with both rain and sweat, the brute became practically uncontrollable and the negotiation of the second jump became for me, an impossibility. I put her at it some half dozen times, and she refused each time, and as the other nags, or what was left of them were coming round the second time I had no alternative but to retire somewhat ingloriously.

After receiving many commiserations - we refreshed ourselves, liberally at The Salisbury, Hertford, and later at The Ridgeway Country Club until the early hours, I only enjoyed myself in a mild sort of way. The wild sort of evening that some of the London Ladies call enjoyment takes some assimilation to the northern mind.

The day was notable for just one other thing. I heard the cuckoo for the first time this year.

Tuesday, May 1st, 1934.

My hitherto troubled finances, I think, are turning the corner. I felt distinctly brighter after I discharged my obligation to Bill. I sent him my cheque yesterday, with a nice little note, and a small gift of a crepe handkerchief, with his initials embroidered thereon just to show my appreciation.

Friday, May 11th, 1934.

The first heat wave of the year. So armed with a book, I spend my luncheon hour 'neath the welcome shade of Kirkstall Abbey, thus providing a happy diversion in the middle of the day. In the evening I went down to Newlaithes and put in a couple of useful hours with spade and barrow.

Noel is launching out for himself now starting to manufacture... "Radiosetz." ...Good luck to him.

Monday, May 21st, 1934. Whitsuntide

The Summer's pleasant pageant begins.

A week, in which all manner of jaunts and jollities are fading into yesterday. It started with the holidays when I set sail with Pat in his vintage Jowett for Runswick Bay, and where I spent four very happy days. We spent most of our time going for long walks... along the rocky beach and up the cliffs to Kettleness and back along the cliffs. Early one morning, five o'clock to be exact, Teddy C. and myself went out with Tom Patton to collect his Lobster pots. It was a brilliant morning... with that sparkling clarity that is peculiar to the east coast. Contrary to the general expectation I did not have a headache; the French name for that headache is mal-de-mer. In all, our catch totalled about 200 crabs, and some half a dozen lobsters. The smell of stale fish in those cobbles was so indescribably pungent that it literally made one gasp for breath. I returned from Runswick by train - filled with the usual type of holiday crowd, so I removed my goods and chattels to comparative privacy of a 'first', and arrived in Leeds in quite a pleasant frame of mind.

On Wednesday evening I had a quiet but pleasant evening's ride... trotting in style to the pub at Esholt, where we regaled ourselves with the odd jar. I came to the conclusion that one of the best ways of enjoying a cigar, is to smoke it in the cool of the evening, jogging homeward along leafy lanes, and twisted byways, through the woods and through the fields. And what contentment descends as the freshness and colour of the early spring mingle with the twilight, and which is only to be surpassed by the sparkling contrast of the early Autumn tints.

Thursday (24.v.34), I took french leave and went with Bill to an "At Home" of the R.A.F. at Catterick Camp. After having had a snack at The Three Greyhounds at Boroughbridge. I must say I was greatly surprised at the licence given to the general public at these military 'At Homes'. I, for instance clambered in and out and over the 'planes almost at will. Came to the conclusion that men serving in His Majesty's Services have a damn good time of life. There are two squadrons with a personnel of about 180 at Catterick.

Friday evening saw me peacefully gardening at both Woodbottom, and Newlaithes, which I followed with a dip in the pool. The water was so cold that I hardly knew whether I was Cuthbert or Cathleen, when I came out!

Yesterday, Bill played cricket with the Old Leos 'an' Eleven against Burnt Yates. And as the team included the local Robert [policeman], the pub served ale all the afternoon. A happy example of rural England. All the same I am unable to comprehend why people will sit so long watching other folk hit balls across a neatly mown field for others to bring them back...

Where is the fun?

Sunday, May 27th, 1934.

At last, I can proudly boast myself to be a true and genuine Yorkshireman. Bill, Charles, and myself achieved Yorkshire's three highest peaks... Ingleborough, Whernside, and Penyghent in twenty-four hours. Here is our Log:

Left Clapham 9.35 (a.m.)

Ingleborough Summit 10.57

Hill Inn 11.39

Whernside Summit 12.50

Left Whernside 1.0

Ribblehead 1.52

Left Ribblehead 2.12

Penyghent Summit 5.10

Horton (The Crown) 6.15

Left Horton 8.20

Arrive Clapham 10.30

Thus the three peaks were accomplished in eight hours walking time just. With a total walking time of 10 hours 10 minutes. I am informed on the authority of Mr. Brown, The President of The Yorkshire Ramblers, that it is equivalent to walking some 35/40 miles on the level.

There are few colourings to add. The weather was fair. The views from the summits were, in the main, disappointing, as we were shrouded in cloud. I was very surprised at my remaining energy when we reached the car.

July 8th, 1934. [Sunday]

I simply cannot let my fortnight's stay at Bill Irwin's flat in Roundhay slip by without some comment. It has been altogether topping. The only summer that comes up to it is way back in '21, when I was at Southcliffe, and those were golden days without a doubt. Some old boy made the wise-crack "...that the golden age was never the present"; so what will this Summer become when it fades into the past and is only a memory?

We have got on amazingly well, believe me, our repartee is, at times, startlingly bright and brisk. I have appreciated, too, his generosity in letting me have the Alvis *[a British car]*. It has been quite like old times to be able to say to one's self, Oh, I'll slip round and see so and so - then just go and do it.

A rapid ciné review of June, sees me at Burley Mills presenting the prizes at The Sports and saying "...a few words" (incidentally quite successfully). Another is my visit with my Headingley Aunts to Colonel Whitworth's place at Nun Monkton. What Gardens, and what weather! Those pleasant evening's playing golf with Bill, Duncan and Lewis... quite like old times. Then those bathing parties at Newlaithes. And those evening rides with Jack K., Ronald, and John H. over the moors to "Dick Hudson's". The balmy smell of the June evenings, but crispened by the moorland breeze together with the companionship of Youth go a long way to make life more liveable.

That excursion to The New Inn at Eccup on horseback was really very amusing. Then the Gymkhana at Rawdon where I got very fed up and peeved at not winning a prize. I am quite sure in my own mind that I was a good second in the 'leaping'. Why the devil must it go to a slip of a girl, just because it is a charity show, and a girl prize-winner appeals to the public fancy?

Then that supper party to The Morritt Arms at Greta Bridge, and the pleasantness of sitting in the gardens of "The Grove" supping one's coffee, and idly scanning "The Tatler" and generally forgetting the worries of the work-a-day world.

I have yet to overcome those panicky qualms regarding Mr. Bruce and Joppa. The state of tedium continues. For nearly four months now, Bruce has not sent me out travelling. Not that I particularly am anxious, because with the general lack of backing up, and the complete absence of responsibility, I've come to the conclusion that I do myself more harm than good in representing a reputed reputable firm, when one's hands are so tied. Youth will always respond to responsibility.

Two glaring examples: The first, over Isle's order which Bruce himself mucked up, and then Turner's order for a sample score [20] special Spilt Hides which Bottomley went and messed up by sending inferior hides, which was a very dirty trick. I learned my lesson. But I ask you, isn't this petty jealousy too utterly ridiculous for words?

Old Mr. Harold Nickols, whilst he admittedly never praised anybody, but, so I'm told, could always tell when he was satisfied. Anyway he always backed up his staff through thick and thin. For instance, if any yard man came to him with a grouse; he'd always listen, but never give judgement, and always refer him back to his foreman, even if the man got the sack, the old man would stick by that. Of course, if the foreman was wrong... he got a hell of a ticking off, but never in public.

In the warehouse I have taken the line of least resistance... to the detriment of my character. It is often on the tip of my tongue to tell Billy Baily what the hell its got to do with him as to how or when I shall work, but as his opinion counts for very little, it doesn't really matter.

Anything for a peaceful life. I have now schooled myself into taking my pleasures gently, and I am not disappointed if nothing happens at all. A sort of mellowing you see. A couple of years ago, if things didn't happen as I wanted 'em... the four walls and roof wouldn't hold me.

So we'll say everything happens for the best.

Monday, July 16th, 1934.

An incident happened this afternoon worthy of record. One of those trivialities, that sets one to think furiously.

On the occasion was Mr. Crooks (Huddersfield) visit to Joppa. In the first place lets get Mr. Cook clear. He is a man for whom I have nothing but the warmest admiration. When only a young fellow of about twenty, he was left with both a bankrupt business and parents on his hands. Eventually after a hell of a struggle he paid off all the creditors twenty shillings in the pound, and has established a highly prosperous business for himself. He has half a dozen grand lads. Incidentally, he was my first customer at Joppa, he has always displayed a very fatherly attitude towards me and which has been duly reciprocated, with the nett result that we have got on remarkably well together.

On his way out this afternoon, we had a few moments together. Now for sometime past he has been fully aware of my difficulties at Joppa, and he suddenly mentioned the proposed amalgamation with Wm. Sykes of Horbury, and adding that if he saw a ghost of a chance of an opening for me it was mine; then ended as abruptly as he began, with a quotation from Kipling.

"Why look at the legs of a peacock, when he has such lovely feathers." is my quotation, however.

Wednesday, July 28th, 1934. Runswick Bay

A real family holiday, and what a bore.

Strangely enough it is the first time for about four years that we have put up with each other's company under the same roof for so long as a fortnight, and under the circumstances, I think it best to pass over the events, and their reactions lightly. It is hardly for me to criticise my parents. Perhaps, of late years, I have become too independent, with the characteristic waywardness of Youth, to think seriously of a home-life with my parents. Today it is impossible.

Grannie was perfectly right, when she called me over the coals the other day, and said that I was getting too self-satisfied, and that I was not half such a nice boy I was a few years ago. "Remember," she continued, "you cannot afford to let people think idly of you. You have your way to make in the world".

Tuesday, August 21st, 1934.

Spent a thoroughly enjoyable evening Rough shooting over part of Bill's six hundred acres at Middleton - 'midst high winds and driving rain, and good company. We were six guns strong, Bill, Charles, Duncan, myself, Leslie M., and Rodney Moore, who is one of the finest devil-may-care, and happy-go-lucky types of Englishmen that I have ever met. On the whole our bag was pretty poor, but it was great fun.

Afterwards, we made our way to The Listers Arms, where metaphorically speaking, we loosened our girths and indulged in something a little stronger than milk.

Monday, August 27th, 1934.

One must make an entry of today's date... Winston Hartley has been moved by his Bank to South Shields.

I have had his duties thrust upon my ox-like shoulders. It may now be said, and with some justification, that I am the head skiv and bottle washer of The Bohemians.

I do not feel particularly cheerful at the prospect of anything at the moment, for I am enveloped in one of those foul fits of despondency. The cause for this depression is the reaction between the real friendliness that Bruce showed towards me last week, when Bottomley was away, and on his return, Bruce's reverse.

When I'm feeling like this I sometimes query the wisdom of my 'eat-drink-and-be-merry,-for-tomorrow-we-may-die' sort of attitude towards life. Is it wise to have tasted the lascivious luxury? Who can foretell the future? Is it better never to have tasted them, than to have their memories haunting you?

September 20th, 1934. *[Thursday]*

For general utility purposes I have decided to buy a small car. But the worst of small cars, as the Frenchman said "...you are too near the accident".

We have decided to christen her Belinda, as she is an old Bull-nosed Morris, of the 1926 vintage. Perhaps to call her "Marie" would be more suitable, but then I don't pretend to be a humorist. The car cost only £3.0.0. *[£255 adj. 2023]* We'll have some fun out of her 'ere long. And we did.

October 23rd, 1934. *[Tuesday]*

My twenty-fifth Birthday.

What have I to show for my first twenty-five years on this earth?... Good health, a zest for life, a sound job, with ample remuneration, the ownership of a car, and rent roll (that sounds so much better than saying that I own a house), and the background of a home life, even if lacking modern comforts is full of Victorian dignity. Then the marvellous friendships, of Bill, Duncan and Lewis, then Dorothy too. The happy satisfaction of seeing my parents settled in Leicester. All this goes to make a contented mind, and to fill one with noble striving. But, alas, that was yesterday.

The realisation that it was all too good to last, only comes when it comes to an end. Thrift is often too late at the bottom of the purse. My occasional lapses into mediocre are very insignificant when compared with life as a whole.

A month ago today, I received a very pathetic little note from Dad. He has been asked to resign his post in Leicester.

Throughout by boyhood, and youthhood, I have dreamed of living a big life, and of doing great and lofty things. My somewhat inglorious career at Wrekin, if nothing else, made me conscious of my mistakes, and gave me zeal to accomplish these things, but now they are as fickle dreams that fade with the breaking of the dawn.

I have always striven to cultivate the habit of taking long views - my own views, independent of those of other folk. But I can foresee myself becoming a mere tooth in the vast mesh of the cog wheels in the machine of life... never to rise above human imbecility, and spending the rest of my days being just a brilliant nobody.

Father is nearer sixty than fifty, and the possibility of his ever working again is, to me, very remote, and it will evolve upon my shoulders to be the family's breadwinner.

I am not so ignorant of history that I misinterpret the actions of great men. Surely it is obvious that Caesar moulded his people as a potter his clay. With such men life becomes as a watch in the hands of a watchmaker. A potter most becomes the objective of my striving.

I have an uphill task before me. Please God give me the necessary strength of purpose, and tact to do it gracefully!

Appendix i

THE RISE AND FALL OF NEW LAITHES, HORSFORTH

According to Edward Parsons in his "History of Leeds"(1834) Volume 1 - Pages 214/5

"...New Laithes, Horsforth was long the residence of Wyomarus Greenwode, 'Cater' to Empress Maude in 1154, and was built in a most beautiful situation on a sheltered and wooded eminence above the River Aire. The prospect down the valley to Kirkstall would have been truly delightful..."

The name 'New Laithes' has its roots in agriculture, and is derived from new leys or pastures, for although it was surrounded by woods, there was some very good agricultural land, well drained and productive to the north and west.

New Laithes was part of the manor of Horsforth - Horse Ford in olden times - for one could only cross the river on horseback. Horseforth does get a mention in Doomsday Book, and was owned along with other vast tracts of land in all three Ridings of Yorkshire by one Robert de Bruis, and from whom the celebrated Bruce's of Scotland were descended. The manor of Horsforth including New Laithes was acquired at a very early stage, probably before the year 1200 by the Abbots of Kirkstall Abbey.

Exactly how and for what purpose New Laithes was used, and for the next 300 years nothing is known.There is no reference of any sort to New Laithes in what records survived from Kirkstall Abbey.

However, as it is barely 2 miles - i.e. 35 minutes pleasant walk from the Abbey, it could have had many uses. But there can be no doubt that they were both very closely linked. It is interesting to note that the old drainage system at New Laithes was of exactly the same construction as those at Kirkstall Abbey - 18 inches wide and 12 inches deep.

About the year 1250 the monks of Kirkstall Abbey started a Forge almost midway between the Abbey and New Laithes, which after 700 years is still producing Iron and Steel castings and forgings.

The real history of New Laithes begins with the dissolution of the Monasteries by Henry VIII in November 1539. The Crown granted all lands held by Kirkstall Abbey to Archbishop Cranmer, who in turn passed them onto his eldest son Thomas, who then sold the manor of Horsforth, including New Laithes to:-

Samuel Green, Stephen Pasley,
Richard Pollard, John Stanhope,
and Robert Craven.

It was at this period that the Greenwood family came to be associated with New Laithes, and indeed it remained with them for the next 250 years. They must have had a great affection for the property for twice during the 250 years they sold New Laithes and bought it back again. Records are in existence showing that James Greenwood, who served as a soldier during the wars between the Dutch and the Spaniards, sold the estate of New Laithes in 1658 and conveyed it to James Lord Viscount Saville, Earl of Sussex, and it was reconveyed back to James Greenwood in 1670.

And again in 1699 the estate was sold to John Swaine of Horsforth, and once again it was reconveyed back, to Joseph Greenwood, in 1728. I myself, as a boy remember being shown the Deeds for these various transactions by Captain Noel Kent-Lemon, who came to live at New Laithes after my parents had left in 1926. I remember being so impressed not only with the size and quality of writing on the parchments but also with the gigantic size of the seals.

In about 1810 or 1812 New Laithes was completely rebuilt, and its status elevated to that of "New Laithes Hall". In a local history of the time it was described as:

"...a commodious and respectable mansion with well laid out pleasure gardens and well-wooded parkland."

The only visible reminder of the original house were to be seen in the cellars which had some fine old stone arches in the traditional Norman pattern (again similar to those still to be seen in the Chapter House at Kirkstall Abbey).

I have in my possession an old coloured print by M. Dubourg circa 1840 and inscribed "New Laithes Hall, near Leeds - Charles Greenwood Esquire".

The road from Horsforth to Bramley, Stanningley and Bradford was indeed immensely circuitous and difficult, but in 1819 an Iron bridge was erected over the River Aire just below New Laithes Hall, and the tempo of life must have changed quite dramatically. Woollen Mills, Dye works, Fellmongers and a Tannery (which belonged to my grandfather) all came into being along the banks of the river, and much of the rural atmosphere of New Laithes must have been destroyed and still later the construction of the railway between the river and New Laithes Hall must have completed the process. So much for the advance of Industry?!

New Laithes Hall did boast of a secret passage. Legend had it that the monks could reach the Abbey by way of the secret underground passage, but that must be accepted as only a pretty legend. As a boy I have been down the passage many, many times. It had a semi-circular stone roof, said to have dated from the 12th century (but I think it was constructed considerably later), and was 4'6" high. The generally accepted theory is that the passage was used by the monks as a secret escape tunnel from the cellars to a distance of about 400 yards from the Hall.

I am a little hazy as to the exact dates of what happened next in the history of New Laithes Hall as all the people who could have told me (and I am now 78) have died, but so far as I can remember from hearsay is that New Laithes Hall passed out of the Greenwood family somewhere between 1860 and 1890, and that the Eastwood family came to live at New Laithes Hall, but whether as owners or as tenants I cannot say.

In about 1890 the Hall was severely damaged by fire. In fact I've heard my father say that most of the interior was gutted.

The Hall was then bought by Mr John Cross who was Deputy Lieutenant for the West Riding of Yorkshire. He rebuilt the Hall and in so doing divided it into two houses. Mr and Mrs Cross lived in one half, which included the main entrance and staircase, a fine series of reception rooms and the former library.

My parents lived in the other half (as tenants) which included the original dining room, breakfast room, billiards room and the ballroom in which some 200 people could dance quite comfortably. I'm afraid we used it for playing badminton!! We also had the benefit of all the old kitchens etc. Each house had gardens and woodlands of about 6 or 7 acres.

I always remember as a boy the great excitement caused when Mr and Mrs Cross invited Lady Astor to stay at New Laithes. Police were everywhere. I thought it was just great!!

Mr Cross died in 1925 and the whole of New Laithes passed to his daughter Marjorie and her husband Captain Noel Kent-Lemon. They were both close friends of mine and I was a frequent visitor to New Laithes Hall right up to the war in 1939.

I was abroad for the entire war and on my return, married and came to live in this part of Yorkshire. In the meantime both Marjorie and Noel had died. *[From a hand-written note in the margin: 'They had a son called Peter, but I believe he died young but not before marrying and having a son also called Peter who I believe lives in the south and I regret we have lost touch.']* I paid what I had hoped would be a nostalgic visit to 'the old home'. However, imagine my dismay to find the entire Hall and outbuildings completely demolished to make way for a modern, very third rate housing estate.

There is not a single trace of either the Hall and the once-lovely gardens to be seen today. All very, very sad.

Parts of the old Manor House, however, which is minute when compared with the Hall still stands on a site just behind where the Hall stood. Parts date back to the 12th century and there is some nice panelling to be seen.

Tim Thackray

October 1987

The Hedges, Thornton-Le-Dale, Pickering

Photo Gallery

Photos of Tim as a young boy. (Centre photo Tim aged 2 in 1911 with Hector)

Photos of Tim: Left 1935/Right 1938

Southcliffe School, Filey. 1922

The Charlton Arms Hotel (now a private residence)

Wrekin College

Wrekin College Chapel

You can still walk down Constitution Hill in Wellington.

Overgrown shooting range on the Ercall where Tim managed to get out of school

Painting of 'New Laithes' where Tim's parents used to live.

(All pictures copyright of S G Liddle)

Appendix ii

THACKRAY - A HISTORY

Thackray

Thackrey

Thackwray

Thackeray

Thackrah

Thackra

Thackoray

Thackera

Thackara

Thackwra

For the ordinary mass of people in England the use of surnames did not begin until about 1250 or 1300. Certainly in the North they were not common until well after 1300. Originally a man's name was his homestead, his village, or even his area - that is to say his address.

I am fully aware that Mr. I. Nichols in his well researched book "The Herald and Genealogist" would have us believe that our ancestors were of French extraction, and came over withKing William in 1066, or shortly after. I think that he basest his on extracts from "The Memorials of the

Abbey of St.Mary at Fountains" by Richard Walbram, which tells us of a Johannes De Thackwra who was Abbot and had the Convent at Fountains where he was a learned and respected man.

But by far the more likely alternative is to be found in Gordon Thackrah's scholarly treatise "The Thackrah Sagabok", who maintains that the root name is very much earlier - going back indeed to Scandinavian times - about 700 A.D. This is by virtue of the many place names in Cumbria with THACK or VRA - THWAITE being the old Norse name for a place cleared of growing wood, or a settlement. And all within an area bounded by old Roman Roads, with Carlisle in the North, Penrith in the east, Whitehaven in the West, and Lake Windermere in the South.

In the areas between Carlisle, Penrith and Whitehaven there are no less than 3 Hamlets/Districts/or Villages by the name of Thackthwaite, and 1 Thackmore. In the area of Cockermouth there is a Thackray Wood, a Thackray Beck, a Setrah Hill, and a Wray Farm, whilst a little further South towards Windermere there is a Dockray, Rownah Whinneray, Keldray, and a Strangrah.

Phonetically all these indicate a "vra" or a "Thack".

Then later, very much later, to Claro, the present area around Harrogate.

In broad outline the Northern half of this area is indeed very similar to that of Norway - so for the early Norse settlers, it would have been rather like home from home!

From about 750 A.D. these Vikings developed a remarkable degree of Culture - a visit to the Viking Museum in York will bear this out. But it is equally apparent that owing to the barren nature of the land, and steepness of the mountains, much of the land was not capable of much cultivation, so as the population increased, the younger sons began to look elsewhere for a living, and thus began their migration south-wards to the more fertile parts of the West Riding, to the district of Claro (Now Harrogate, Ilkley, Wetherby, even to the outskirts of the present Leeds).

Another possible, in fact a more probable reason for this migration, was their wish to escape the continual harassment by the Picts and Scots from the North.

These conditions led to the final flowering of the Viking Age. Their greatest achievement was the development and perfection of their ocean going Longboats, which was probably the most potent war weapon known to man until the invention of gunpowder. Make no mistake - this was a technological development of the first magnitude, for it enabled them to explore (and exploit) the whole of the Western world from the Mediterranean to America. This in due course led to the development of a large international trade. Thus began a complex sort of culture (as distinct from a civilisation), which altered the face of the world.

The popular image of the Vikings as exclusively plundering pirates is entirely false - another of those stupid little fallacies that find their way into popular belief.

Technically they were most skilful in metalwork, including weapons, builders of ships, and navigation. They were intellectually brilliant, with law-making of the highest order... and from which all parliaments have sprung. They were, however, a restless people - as restless as the Atlantic by which they lived.

The effect of the Vikings on the Western world has been greatly underestimated - and often ignored in History, but they contributed much and deserve better appreciation.

I hope that I have put forward my arguments with sufficient clarity to convince you that it is far and away more likely that the name of Thackray is old Norse and that our origins are in fact Scandinavian and not French.

The prefix "De" does not necessarily constitute or indicate a French or Norman origin.

As every schoolboy (or girl) knows that "De" in French means "of", so a Johannes de Thackwra merely means John of Thackwra. ie his home or his district.

At the time of The Doomsday Survey in 1086, Cumbria was considered to be something of an outpost, to the point of being a small but separate Kingdom from England. The Survey shows Fewston to be uninhabited, and Hampsthwaite doesn't even get a mention. The word

Hampsthwaite is pure Scandinavian, being derived from "Hama" - a home or small-holding and "thwaite", as already mentioned, being a place cleared of growing wood. Much later, in medieval times Hampsthwaite did become quite a populous market town.

The nearby district of Fountains in Nidderdale is probably one of the most elegant and beautiful places to be found anywhere in Yorkshire, and it was here at Fountains that the Cistercian order of Monks decided to found their Monastery, shortly after 1100 A.D. Owing to their industry it was not long before they controlled (or owned outright), vast areas of wild and magnificent moorland which provided ideal conditions for the rearing and grazing of sheep. In fact so did it prosper that within 150 years it was to become one of the great wool centres in the country. The early Thackrays must have been a wily old lot for they were quick to appreciate that if they became connected with the Monastery at Fountains in any way - not only did they enjoy both legal and political protection from the Monks, but, and by far and away more important, they became free of feudal obligations ie. soldiering, and other irksome duties which might be required of them had they been tenants of one of the great landowners ie. the Nobility. The Monks of the Cistercian orders were both strict and puritan in outlook, and from which the early Thackrays must have learned much, and which perhaps accounts for that streak which has come through in so many generations.

From this time on, ie the 13th Century, there are surprisingly frequent written references to Thackwras. The first being in 1378 and comes from a Poll Tax Return in the reign of King Richard II, when they were one of several local families who had no alternative but to contribute to the obnoxious Taxes ...three shillings and fourpence...!! (a lot of money in those days!) to enable King Richard to carry on with the miserable French wars.

The next mention is in 1391 when a Nicholas de Thackwra was tenant of 31 acres of "goode farm lande at Fountains". And ten years later (in 1401) there was a William de Thackwra - yeoman - who was tenant of 20 acres at Fountains. William must have prospered for the reference continues "...and later was known to have kept The Grange at Hayshay, near Hartwith, Harrogate (Hayshay, alas, not in existence today).

In 1453 under the Will of Elena Fulford of York - Joan Thackwra (note the dropping of the French style "de") was to receive her work box and her jewels.

During a survey made towards the end of the reign of Queen Elizabeth in about 1600 it shows that there were 14 Thackray families (in various forms of spelling) living in the area covered by the villages of Walshford, Wetherby,

Bramham, Brimham Tockwith, Hunsingore, Ramsgill, Knaresborough, Ripon, and Hampsthwaite.

From this time on, when Parish Registers first made their appearance the name of Thackray in one or other of its many and various spellings is quite frequent. It is interesting to note that they were concentrated in such a small piece of Yorkshire roughly covered by the Washburn Valley and Nidderdale to the north and Wharfedale and Airedale in the south.

Little heed should be paid to these various spellings. In the Parish registers of Hunsingore there are two separate examples where the spellings changed during the individual's life. Ann Thackray, (formally Whincup), the second wife of William Thackray, was married in 1801 as Thackray - and yet buried as Thackwray - and Mary was christened as Thackery in 1822 yet buried as Thackray in 1826.

So much for the phonetic spelling as against the written word.

Sooner or later the question is bound to arise - Are we, in any way, related to, perhaps the most famous of our clan - William Makepeace Thackeray? The answer to this is both "yes" and "no" because there is absolutely no evidence of any direct relationship or connection, but on the other hand "yes" because we all have come from the same small area of Yorkshire, which I have already mentioned - so going back a few centuries it is not unreasonable to suppose that we all came from the same stock.

There is a record of a Walter Thackray or Thackeray living in Hampsthwaite together with his wife Margaret in the early 1600s. For the Parish Register shows that Margaret died in 1609 and Walter in 1618. Their grandson Thomas was born in 1628, and he in turn had a son (don't laugh!) called Timothy and who became the Parish Clerk, and it is indeed recorded that many of his descendants held that office.

Now Timothy had a brother who rejoiced in the name of Elias. He must have been a diligent lad for he became the Rector of Hauxwell in North Yorkshire, where he died unmarried in 1737.

But going back to Timothy, he had a son called Thomas, who was baptised at Hampsthwaite on December 8th. 1693. At a very early age this young man evinced a scholarly aptitude - no doubt helped by his Uncle Elias. He took up teaching as a profession. He must have been a man of some presence and character for ultimately he became Headmaster of Harrow School in 1746. Later he was made a Doctor of Divinity, and became Archdeacon of Surrey.

He died in 1760.

It appears that he begat a large family, the exact number not being known. But he thereby established the name of Thackeray in the south of England. (From here onwards there is a family pedigree given in The Herald and Genealogist of 1864.)

Now, the youngest son of Archdeacon Thackeray was (the first) William Makepeace who spent his life in India in the Indian Civil Service. He died in 1815. His grandson also bearing exactly the same name, was to become the celebrated Author and Novelist. Thackeray the Novelist died in Bayswater, London, in 1863 at the early age of 53. His wife Isobella was the daughter of Colonel Shawe of the Indian Army and died very many years later in 1894 at Leigh in Essex.

The old Thackeray Home in Hampsthwaite was pulled down around 1890.

Let us turn to our branch of the Thackrays. It is not known when they first came and settled at Lund House, Hunsingore, or indeed exactly where they came from.

But Mrs. Dent of Rilston Hall has with very great kindness gone to a lot of trouble in looking up (and in some cases deciphering) old records and Deeds concerning both Lund House, and the Thackray connection with the property. The first written record is in (about, as exact document is undated) 1300 when it was known as La Londe.

Lund House was indeed part of the Rilston Estate and the Goderyke family - but for convenience let me use the modern spelling of Goodwick, but it passed into the ownership of the Petre family (there is no record as to how) in 1560 or thereabouts. The Hon. E. Petre sold it to Lord Stourton.

Mr. Dent has in his possession the Auctioneer's Catalogue dated 1832, which describes Lund House as "...a farm in good heart and let to Mr. W. Thackray, an excellent tenant"!

The earliest mention of a Thackray is in a Rilston Estate Audit Book of 1826 when a Henry(?) Thackray was tenant of an Inn, a smithy, and some land at Cattal.

There is also a reference to another Thackray at Little Rilston in the 1830's.

The Parish Registers at Hunsingore did not start until 1626 and for the first 20 years are completely illegible and mildewed.

Hunsingore must have been a very small and unimportant hamlet for there were only 16 marriages recorded between the years of 1697 and1744.

It is wishful thinking to suppose that the early Thackrays were Yeoman Farmers, but there is no documentary evidence to support this, and there is a massive collection of Deeds and documents in the Archives of Rilston Hall - probably one of the most extensive collections still remaining in private ownership, that is to say in the possession of the Dent family. It dates, believe it or not, from 1217. So we must assume that the early Thackrays at Hunsingore were tenant, and not yeoman, farmers.

Unfortunately there is absolutely no trace of the Old Hall at Hunsingore - nor can its site be fixed with any degree of certainty. In fact there are really no old houses left in Hunsingore today. I always have a sense of disappointment whenever we motor through the village. Even Lund House was rebuilt when the Thackrays left and moved to Cobble Hall on the outskirts of Leeds. Cobble Hall was a fine House with some 200 acres of good agricultural land. It is now a Golf Course, but the House, or at least parts of it, form the present Club House.

I think it is fairly obvious that we were as a family very closely connected with the Walshford, Hunsingore, Rilston areas for several generations.

And so I feel a few remarks on the History of Rilston Hall might be of interest, as it is so bound up with the Knights Templars. To describe the Knights Templars in just a couple of words ...they were "warrior monks." These knights of St. John of Jerusalem who often became known as "the soldiers of The Red Cross" because of the blood-red Cross worn on the left breast of their white habit.

Hence, of course the beginnings of "The Red Cross" which has served mankind for over a thousand years.

The story of these "religious-cum-military monks" is interesting. About 300 A.D. the Empress Helena, mother of Constantine the Great, discovered the tomb of the Holy Sepulchre at Jerusalem. And over the site of the sacred tomb erected a large and beautiful Church - the Church of the Holy Grail. Almost at once pilgrims from far and wide started to pay their respects. Very soon this became "big business". And as one might expect, this in turn was followed by rivalries, bribery, hostility, even murder; so much so that the area became one of alternate conquest and surrender, and which in the end culminated in the English Crusades of 1100.

It was owing to the trials and tribulations suffered by the Pilgrims that the Knights Templars came into being. Their hospitals and their houses of entertainment spread rapidly throughout Europe, and very soon they became one of the richest and most powerful organisations in the world. Their duties being to take charge of the highways and guide the pilgrims through difficult passes, through which they had to travel in order to reach the Holy Land, and in general give the Pilgrims protection.

Their vows were strict and included the suppression of infidelity and preserving trust - a rare fortitude in those days.

Not unnaturally with such a background they expanded and prospered greatly. Just to give one instance - King Philip 11 of France in the thirteenth century bequeathed the huge sum of £100,000 to the Templars.

Largely because of the English participation in the Crusades, it was not long before they were well established in England ...and so to Yorkshire.

The De Ros Family, from France, came into the possession of the Rilston Estates in 1170, which included the Manors of both Hunsingore and Walshford. The original Charter - still in the Dent Collection at Rilston Hall, but unfortunately undated, however thought to be 1217. The charter was later confirmed by Henry III.

The De Ros Family gave Rilston to the Knights Templars, and thus strengthened by Royal perogative, they soon became established, and developed their influence on local affairs. Progressing in both wealth and power it was only a matter of time before jealousies developed. (Just in passing, it was the Templars who built the original Castle at Helmsley).

The Manors of Rilston, Walshford, and Hunsingore reverted to the Crown during the reign of King Henry VII. In 1542 King Henry VIII sold the entire estate to Henry Goderyke. He appears to have been an excellent landlord. This family held the estate for some 300 years, until 1833, when Sir James Goderyke, the seventh baronet, died without issue.

The Rílston Estate was then sold to Joseph Dent - landed gentry from the Dales who (in 1987) still own the property. They were indeed the landlords to the Thackrays who farmed at Lund House, Hunsingore. There was a James Thackray living at Scotton (between Fewston and Otley) in 1889. The village of Scotton achieved fame as being the home of Guy Fawkes, leader of the Gunpowder Plot - but more of that in a minute. Returning to James Thackray, whose father William Thackray farmed at Monk Ings at Scotton ...In ploughing out some old pasture land some very old, but sound copper-pitchers, steel battle axes and also a curious Iron Firegrate, besides many other ancient fragments, were discovered.

Most of these are deposited in the Museum at York.

But returning to Guy Fawkes. He was born in York on April 16th, 1570. He was educated at St. Pater's School, York, but always spent his holidays at the family home - Scotton Hall.

He seems to have been a young man full of vigour and enterprise, and with a keen and daring spirit. As he grew into manhood he became increasingly under the influence of his Grandfather, who was an ardent Papist. Hence his anger at The Reformation, and his growing dislike of both the Government and of Parliament - so what better way to rid the country of both - by blowing up the Houses of Parliament?

As, of course, everyone knows he was caught red-handed. Poor old Guy was subject to terrible tortures, eventually being hung, drawn and quartered.

In 1700 there was a Thomas Thackray of Hull who became an Alderman of the City of Hull. He was a merchant, and quite wealthy. He had no male issue but two daughters, one of whom married Sir Richard Hildyard, Knight of Beverley - one of the very old aristocratic families of Yorkshire and still very much in existence today - in fact my son Charles went to Bramcote School in Scarborough with one of the Hildyard boys and I played Cricket with Father Hildyard in "The Fathers' Match" at Bramcote, and who claimed that we were relations!!!

The other daughter married a Sir E. Mountford, Knight, but both the family and title are now extinct.

The Parish Registers of Hull give no evidence of his being born or married there - only a record of his burial.

...And so to a final summing up of the background of the Thackrays.

It is always a bit risky to generalise - more so on families, and particularly so on people. But certain characteristics must inevitably emerge.

For many centuries it would indicate that the family livelihood came from farming and the breeding of sheep.

This leads us to the one plain fact over the last 200 years or so where records are available - We have been (and still are) middle-class.

There is no record of any who have attained 'County' status, or were given any titles. The majority enjoyed private education at either Public or Grammar School - but few went to University. On the other hand none have been manual workers such as normally associated with 'the working class'.

From the various Parish Records it would seem that a considerable majority of Thackrays were non-conformists. But no-where is there any record of crime or violence.

There is a love of literature and of culture - a continuance of the old Norse Saga tradition, no doubt. They loved travel, particularly of travel to quiet places off the beaten track - therefore justifying the "wra" in the name - the Viking restlessness for far-away places.

Few have undertaken either public or political service or received decorations for so doing. None appear wealthy, landed, or titled.

And so a picture emerges of a healthy long-lived family of average pragmatic intelligence, peaceful, yet at the same time individualistic - quietly going about their business, be it industry or profession.

I feel we reflect the majority of the qualities, one way or another, which we have spent the last 1000 years in developing - practical, adaptable, dependable, warm and friendly but never glamorous or distinguished.

FINALE

Its really rather sad that after all I have written - this is probably the end of the line so far as the Thackrays are concerned, and in fact almost so far as all our families are concerned. *[We will meet these other families in future volumes.]*

There are no male heirs in the Cheetham Family. The Hardcastles, The Couplands and the Speak Families have already faded into oblivion, and are now only a memory.

The Holdsworths only happen to be connected with the Thackrays because my Father's sister Emily married John Holdsworth in 1913. The Holdsworth family do have an unbroken ancestry right back to 1296, and continues to this day with James Luke Holdsworth, born in 1980 (half Chinese!).

The Elwis Family record is somewhat disjointed but owing to Rupert's fertility there are male children by both his first and second marriages - so the name survives.

As for the Thackrays: ...it now seems unlikely that Colin and Sheila will have any further family (their only child being a girl) and over my son Charles hangs the big question mark? *[unlikely as he is now a retired bachelor]*

My Thanks and References

1.J.G.Nichols "The Herald and Geneologist". Volume II 1865.

British Museum reference No. 2101C re the very early Thackrays

2. "The Thackrah Sagabok"" by Gordon H. Thackrah, Crowthorn End, Edgworth, Bolton, Lancs BL7 OJX 3rd. Edition 1980

3. "Nidderdale and The Garden of the Nidd" - a YorkshireRhineland. By Harry Speight. Published London 1894 byElliot Stock and Co., 62 Paternoster Row, London EC which includes a History of Hunsingore: The Dent Family:also a Family Tree of the Hardcastle Family. I have quoted quite a lot from this Book. See page 340 for a fuller description of the finds made on William Thackray's land at Scotton in 1889.

4. "The Memorials of The Abbey of St. Mary of Fountains" byJohn Richard Walbram (pages 343, 389, 409, 418)

5. "Nobilitas Sola Virtus" see pages 315, 440, 451, 557 re Thomas Thackray of Hull

6. From the General Census of both 1841 and 1871

7. Please see The Archives Department at The Sheepscar Library, Leeds. The Index of Wills and Inventories. This gives full details of all the early Thackrays right back to 1678 and up to 1800.

8. And, of course, my most sincere thanks to Adrian Phillips - who married Elizabeth Thackray. He must have gone to enormous trouble to ferret out and check all the various dates.

Thanks, again, Adrian.

Printed in Great Britain
by Amazon

41299461R00129